Education, Authority, and the Critical Citizen

This book offers a unique analysis of the tension between the individual and society in educational contexts, and the role that citizenship and democratic education can play. It approaches the question from two different perspectives – the institutional and the interactional – and argues that any solution must answer the tension from both or it will necessarily fail. The answer is found through a political methodology that places education at the centre and concludes that a balance can be found if we embrace the federated disestablishment of education and state and internally democratic schooling that aims to realise the emancipation of the political child.

The book situates itself in the tradition of political philosophy that is education focused, identifying an unresolved tension between the individual and society in the works of Rousseau, Dewey, and Freire. It discusses the concept of authority as a primary issue persisting in this tension. It does so by exploring both interactional and institutional responses based on the idea of the free individual and cooperative associations. The author advocates an education system that creates the necessary space for the cultivation of the free individual and is run by the principles of internally democratic schooling.

With a strong focus on citizenship and the role of education in the development of social justice-oriented citizens, this book will be of great interest to researchers, academics, and postgraduate students in the fields of philosophy of education, political philosophy, educational theory, and citizenship education.

Neil Wilcock is an Honorary Research Fellow at Birkbeck College, University of London. His research interests have come to focus on the intersection between philosophy and educational theory. This has manifested as research into the methodology of political philosophy seen through the lens of education and allowed him to explore shared concepts within their framework, such as authority and freedom.

New Directions in the Philosophy of Education Series

Series Editors

Michael A. Peters, Beijing Normal University, China

Gert Biesta, Maynooth University, Ireland and University of Edinburgh, UK

Liz Jackson, The University of Hong Kong, Hong Kong

Marek Tesar, The University of Auckland, New Zealand

This book series is devoted to the exploration of new directions in the philosophy of education. After the linguistic turn, the cultural turn, and the historical turn, where might we go? Does the future promise a digital turn with a greater return to connectionism, biology, and biopolitics based on new understandings of system theory and knowledge ecologies? Does it foreshadow a genuinely alternative radical global turn based on a new openness and interconnectedness? Does it leave humanism behind or will it reengage with the question of the human in new and unprecedented ways? How should philosophy of education reflect new forces of globalisation? How can it become less Anglo-centric and develop a greater sensitivity to other traditions, languages, and forms of thinking and writing, including those that are not rooted in the canon of Western philosophy but in other traditions that share the "love of wisdom" that characterises the wide diversity within Western philosophy itself. Can this be done through a turn to intercultural philosophy? To indigenous forms of philosophy and philosophising? Does it need a post-Wittgensteinian philosophy of education? A post-postmodern philosophy? Or should it perhaps leave the whole construction of "post"-positions behind?

In addition to the question of the intellectual resources for the future of philosophy of education, what are the issues and concerns that philosophers of education should engage with? How should they position themselves? What is their specific contribution? What kind of intellectual and strategic alliances should they pursue? Should philosophy of education become more global, and if so, what would the shape of that be? Should it become more cosmopolitan or perhaps more decentred? Perhaps most importantly in the digital age, the time of the global knowledge economy that reprofiles education as privatised human capital and simultaneously in terms of an historic openness, is there a philosophy of education that grows out of education itself, out of the concerns for new forms of teaching, studying, learning, and speaking that can provide comment on ethical and epistemological configurations of economics and politics of knowledge? Can and should this imply a reconnection with questions of democracy and justice?

This series comprises texts that explore, identify, and articulate new directions in the philosophy of education. It aims to build bridges, both geographically and temporally: bridges across different traditions and practices and bridges towards a different future for philosophy of education.

In this series

Wards a Posthuman Theory of Educational Relationality
Simon Ceder

Bearing with Strangers
Arendt, Education and the Politics of Inclusion
Morten T. Korsgaard

Literature and Philosophical Play in Early Childhood Education
A Humanities Based Approach to Research and Practice
Viktor Johansson

Ilan Gur-Ze'ev and Education
Pedagogies of Transformation and Peace
Alexandre Guilherme

Education, Crisis and Philosophy
Ubuntu within Higher Education
Yusef Waghid

Essays in the Phenomenology of Learning
The Challenge of Proximity
Fiachra Long

Zehou Li and the Aesthetics of Educational Maturity
A Transcultural Reading
Flora Liuying Wei

Nature, Art, and Education in East Asia
Philosophical Connections
Edited by Ruyu Hung

Education, Authority, and the Critical Citizen
Democratic Schooling and the Disestablishment of Education and State
Neil Wilcock

For more information about the series, please visit www.routledge.com/
New-Directions-in-the-Philosophy-of-Education/book-series/NDPE

Education, Authority, and the Critical Citizen

Democratic Schooling and the Disestablishment of Education and State

Neil Wilcock

Routledge
Taylor & Francis Group

LONDON AND NEW YORK

First published 2024
by Routledge
4 Park Square, Milton Park, Abingdon, Oxon OX14 4RN

and by Routledge
605 Third Avenue, New York, NY 10158

Routledge is an imprint of the Taylor & Francis Group, an informa business

© 2024 Neil Wilcock

British Library Cataloguing-in-Publication Data
A catalogue record for this book is available from the British Library

Library of Congress Cataloging-in-Publication Data
Names: Wilcock, Neil, author.
Title: Education, authority, and the critical citizen : democratic schooling and the disestablishment of education and state / Neil Wilcock.
Description: Abingdon, Oxon ; New York, NY : Routledge, 2024. | Series: New directions in the philosophy of education | Includes bibliographical references and index.
Identifiers: LCCN 2023009405 (print) | LCCN 2023009406 (ebook) | ISBN 9781032222691 (hardback) | ISBN 9781032222714 (paperback) | ISBN 9781003271871 (ebook)
Subjects: LCSH: Education and state--United States. | Education--United States--Philosophy. | Education--Aims and objectives--United States. | Democracy and education--United States.
Classification: LCC LC89 .W52 2024 (print) | LCC LC89 (ebook) | DDC 379.73--dc23/eng/20230414
LC record available at https://lccn.loc.gov/2023009405
LC ebook record available at https://lccn.loc.gov/2023009406

ISBN: 978-1-032-22269-1 (hbk)
ISBN: 978-1-032-22271-4 (pbk)
ISBN: 978-1-003-27187-1 (ebk)

DOI: 10.4324/9781003271871

Typeset in Sabon
by SPi Technologies India Pvt Ltd (Straive)

Contents

Acknowledgements

This book has been a labour of love for me, and I hope that it is received warmly by those who do me the favour of dedicating the time to read it. It is important to me to thank those people that have been instrumental in the realisation of this book. First, I would like to thank Gert Biesta and the other series editors, as well as the lovely people at Routledge, for giving me the opportunity to write this book.

I would like to note that the formation of my thought and philosophical outlook has felt at times like an unorthodox swim against a fairly strong current, and yet, I have always felt supported. I am very fortunate in this regard. Most notably, this support has been provided by my supervisors Tommy Lynch, Ruth Mantin, and Susan James but also by the University of Chichester and Birkbeck College who have continued to support my research. I am forever grateful for their interventions, corrections, challenges, and encouragements. I would also like to take the opportunity to thank Ben Colburn, Joshua Forstenzer, and Lisa Herzog for the kindness and advice that you have shown me.

More than anything, I would like to take the opportunity to thank my wife Elena and my daughter Leila, who have put up with more than anyone can reasonably expect for longer than anyone can reasonably ask. I love you both and hope that this book has been worth the sacrifices that you have made for me. I look forward to repaying the favour as we move forward together.

Figure 0.1 Overlooking lake from an island in Viinijärvi, Finland, 1999.

Photo credit: Neil Wilcock, 1999.

Introduction

Background

When I was about sixteen years of age, I concluded that the only coherent answer for a meaningful and free life within a cooperative association must have as its foundation, large-scale voluntary self-education. Of course, I would not have expressed it in this way, but I certainly did try and explain the idea behind the phrase "voluntary self-education" to numerous people who looked at me quite blankly. Part of the problem was that, somewhat understandably, I did not really know what this meant or how it might be realised. All I knew was that it seemed to be the only way that we could find freedom and live in a world where we looked after each other. From what I remember, the reason that I felt this way was because I felt distinctly unfree and unheard, and yet, I knew that I was in a relatively privileged position compared to most people in the world. I reasoned that no rational person would choose to construct the world with so much suffering, so education must be a part of the answer. I knew that people could not be forced to see the suffering and their own part in it, so they must actively seek the knowledge themselves. Lastly, I knew that other people, as they are now, could not be trusted to educate others without coercion because from where do they gain the unquestioned authority to be directing the knowledge of others, so education must be directed by each individual. These thoughts appeared to me to be encapsulated by the phrase, voluntary self-education.

At least, this is the narrative that I recall twenty-five years later and after having spent a good portion of that time thinking about these issues. At the time, I did not know that the thoughts that I was thinking were related to questions that political theorists and philosophers have been engaging with for as long as we have collected together in union. I only knew the injustice that I felt, informed in part because of my misguided teenage angst and in part because of a deeply held sense that I was in some way both a victim of unfairness and a beneficiary of it.

I am fortunate to find myself in a position where I get to write a book about the thoughts that have troubled my mind throughout my adult life.

DOI: 10.4324/9781003271871-1

This book is a manifestation of my relationship with the world. It is in large part a private experience applied to a public problem. It can never represent the full and complete answer because it does not, and cannot, take into consideration the world as it is seen and experienced by others. But I hope that I have seen something through my eyes that is representative of that which you have seen through yours, and maybe together we can begin to move towards some shared aim that will gain focus as we approach it in conversation with each other. I hope further that I have adequately conveyed the thoughts in my head and the words that follow become a part of the discussion on how to find freedom within political association.

Motivation

In this book, I engage in topics and with philosophers that, to a certain extent, have fallen out of fashion, and the arguments that I make are as much an appeal to re-evaluate these ideas, as they are an argument for the conclusions that I draw. I begin with the concept of the citizen, which has not suffered this fate and continues to sit at the centre of our political and educational conversation. From this position, it generates two demanding questions: namely, what form should the citizen take and how is that citizen cultivated in society. I motivate the arguments of this book by pointing out the contemporary significance of these questions. Within the domain of education, I refer to the shifting conceptualisation of the citizen and the role of citizenship education in the United Kingdom that elicited the creation of the Select Committee on Citizenship and Civic Engagement and the publication of their report, 'The Ties That Bind: Citizenship and Civic Engagement in the 21st Century', hereafter referred to as *The Ties That Bind* (2018). Beyond the immediate scope of education, the concept of the citizen maintains contemporary significance. A key example of this is the consequences of the United Kingdom's secession from the European Union and the growing sentiments of anti-immigration and nationalism within the Western political world.

The question of the citizen is complex enough, but it is further complicated when one realises that there exists a tension between the citizen and the society of which they are a part. Answering this tension is the central aim of the book and it is through this tension that the book motivates the positive theses I propose. A clear example of the manifestation of the tension between the individual and society in the political realm is with respect to the state response to the Covid-19 pandemic. A competent and considerate state has to consider the impact that their decisions will have upon the health and welfare of their citizens in a myriad of contexts, these include the context of their immediate health (i.e. chances of contracting and spreading the virus and their chance of survival); the household economy (i.e. how families will continue to have access to basic necessities and the means to afford those necessities); the rights of the citizens (i.e. at the most basic level, how are the rights of equality and freedom maintained but also how to justify the limitation of rights to congregate, to travel, observe religious practices, etc.); and the health of the national economy (due to private interest in the economy, a weak economy directly impacts on the well-being of the individuals and, as a result, must be a consideration also). This is a delicate balance made more difficult by the fact that a prioritisation of one will directly constrain the others. This framing illustrates why it is valuable and fruitful to conduct an exploration into the citizen through the tension between the individual and society.

This book offers an analysis of the tension between the individual and society. This is understood as an ontological tension which I address in a political and educational context. The intention is not to dissolve the tension but to recalibrate it into a positive relationship. This is achieved through a progression of thought which culminates in the defence of internally democratic schooling and the federated disestablishment of education and state. As such, it is situated firmly within a tradition of political philosophy that employs education as a central component, such as that offered by Jean-Jacques Rousseau, John Dewey, and Paulo Freire. The politico-educational projects of Rousseau, Dewey, and Freire form the theoretical foundation of the analysis that is offered.

After establishing the method which I shall employ, I then establish an idea of the aim that I imagine. This is the person that shall inhabit the cooperative association we share, the person that I call the Critical Citizen. From this foundation, I identify the concept of authority as the primary problem that persists within their respective analyses of the tension between the individual and society. I then pursue a positive thesis, which is composed of two interconnected paths. First, I shall identify and defend the pedagogical practice necessary for the realisation of the Critical Citizen, a form of the free individual who retains freedom in the face of the interests and responsibilities that come with cooperative association. Second, I identify and defend a form of cooperative association that minimises the coercion and oppression of the individuals within its dominion while simultaneously cultivating active citizens as its inhabitants. These two arms represent an interactional and an institutional response to the tension between the individual and society, both of which, following Rousseau, are educative in construct and deemed necessary for the resolution of that tension.

Once I have established this position, I make two radical recommendations that are mutually interdependent: one institutional and one interactional. First, I propose that these schools should be run in accordance with the principles of internally democratic schooling, pioneered by the likes of Dewey and A. S. Neill, but which deploys a problem-posing pedagogy influenced by the practise of Freire. Second, I advocate an education system aimed at creating the space necessary for the cultivation of the Critical Citizen, which requires the federated disestablishment of schools. This builds off of the debate that takes place between the defenders of state education such as the liberal philosopher Amy Gutmann and the libertarians and radicals who perceive the coercive force of the state's role, such as Milton Freidman and Ivan Illich. I argue that these two arms, if pursued concurrently, address the coercive force of one's social environment in two meaningful ways. First, they mitigate potentially freedom-constraining aspects of society through the removal of unjustifiable power relations. Second, they render explicit the tension that remains in one's social environment and in one's relationships with others, thereby negating the insidiousness that often accompanies the tension between the individual and society.

Breaking the constellations

In Chapter 1, I shall continue an argument that I have made elsewhere (Wilcock 2021) and argue that a philosophical thread can be traced through the theories of Rousseau, Dewey, and Freire and that doing so provides a space to develop a philosophical methodology, which employs education to resolve the tension between the individual and society. I shall also explain why I have isolated these three thinkers for the development of my argument. I suggest that Rousseau, Dewey, and Freire each engage in politico-educational projects which seek to employ the practice of philosophy as a means to the development of the person and as a method to discover and answer the problems of cooperative associations. Further to this, I argue that the influence of the immediate predecessor in this narrative is felt and observable within each politico-educational project. As such, I argue that it is productive to read Rousseau, Dewey, and Freire in conversation with each other and I use this as the methodological foundation for the arguments that I develop throughout the rest of the book.

In Chapter 2, I identify the aim of education, which I refer to as the Critical Citizen. I employ this term because I believe that it captures the character of the concept. The use of the word "citizen" may be contentious because it could be seen to imply membership to a state, but this need not be the case. The term is used because it is best placed to identify a sense of societal responsibility. The Critical Citizen is drawn out from the interpretations of Rousseau, Dewey, and Freire offered in the previous chapter alongside three prominent models of the citizen: the participatory democratic, the communitarian, and the cosmopolitan conceptions of the citizen. Rousseau, Dewey, and Freire are put into conversation with these three models of the citizen and their influences and overlaps identified. From the analysis that I offer, it is concluded that the citizen that should operate as the end-in-view of education is descriptively communitarian, normatively cosmopolitan, an active participant in one's society, and a possessor of rights and responsibilities.

In Chapter 3, I address the obstacles to the realisation of the model of the individual that operates as the aim of education. This Critical Citizen is defined by its positive relationship between the interests of the individual and the interests of society and so it is necessary to explore the tension that exists between these two groups and what is the root of that tension. I advance the notion that the tension between the individual and society is a problem of authority. Referring back to the works of Rousseau, Dewey, and Freire, I illustrate how the problem of authority manifests within their own politico-educational projects, how they address this problem, and the limitations of their resolutions to the problem of authority.

To this point, the book has aimed to establish several things: the method-ology, which is the politico-educational philosophical approach informed by Rousseau, Dewey, and Freire; the aim, which is the Critical Citizen; and the problem of authority, which is identified as the key component of the tension between the individual and society. The Critical Citizen has the theoretical space to exist if the political structure, both interactional and institutional, is arranged to minimise the coercive force of the tension between the individual and society. From this point forward, the book begins to build its positive thesis on the foundations established by these previous chapters. It is from this point that the two-pronged model of democratic education is developed.

Chapter 4 builds upon the analysis of authority from the previous chapter but within the context of the institutional structure of education. The institu-tional structure of education refers to the ways in which the institutions of society are managed, constructed, and organised in relation to the education of its members and how those institutions relate to the members of society. In seeking a resolution to the tension between the individual and society through the institutional structure of education, I shall focus the analysis of authority specifically within the institutional setting. Therefore, this chapter will address the tension through an exploration into the problem of author-ity. I explore the different conceptualisations of legitimate authority that hold sway in political thought such as those devised by Hannah Arendt, Max Weber, Carl J. Friedrich, and Joseph Raz. Then, I shall apply that analysis within the context of democratic education. In particular, I focus on the lib-eral democratic model offered by Amy Gutmann and the implementation and practice of democratic education in schools in England and Wales following the publication by the Advisory Group on Citizenship of the 'Education for Citizenship and the Teaching of Democracy in Schools' report, hereafter referred to as *The Crick Report* (1998), which led to citizenship education becoming compulsory in England and Wales. However, the institutional structure of education represents only the first prong of the problem of authority and the tension between the individual and society. To be coherent, one must address also the interactional structure of education.

Therefore, following on from the previous chapter, in Chapter 5, I address the second arm of the response to the tension between the individual and soci-ety that is to be read in concert with the institutional structure of education. Where the institutional is concerned with the authoritative voice of the institutions of one's social environment, the interactional is concerned with the authoritative relationship between persons. The interactional is understood as the immediate learning environment with relation to the interaction between the students and the teacher. Therefore, the interactional structure of education is the pedagogy applied in the classroom environment, or more specifically that structure of the immediate learning environment with relation to the interaction between student, teacher, and the curriculum. I transpose the discussion of political authority from the previous chapter into the educational context and clarify how authority is treated and understood in educational theory with a particular focus on the relationships between the students, and between those students and the teacher. I explore competing conceptualisations of the authority of the teacher and the educational practice that is built upon that conceptualisation. This exploration includes R. S. Peters' Weberian analysis that forms the foundation of his analytic philosophy of education and the challenge to authority that often accompanies progressive and radical education such as that described by A. S. Neill and Nigel Wright.

In the final two chapters of this book, I present detailed accounts of the interactional and institutional structures of education that seem best placed to resolve the tension between the individual and society and realise the Critical Citizen. This constitutes two answers, one primarily addressing the interactional concerns and the other primarily addressing the institutional concerns. Two answers that are designed to be pursued in concert and concurrently. How easily the interactional and the institutional branches of a person's philosophical position can come into conflict with one another can be seen in Freire, one of the few people brave enough to make a serious effort to implement his philosophical and pedagogical ideas into society from a position of societal authority. I look at this phenomenon in more detail in a previous publication (Wilcock 2020). In Chapter 6, I argue that the institutional design best placed to support the realisation of the Critical Citizen is the federated disestablishment of education and state. I argue that this is the case because it challenges the coercive control exhibited and sought by unilateral authority claims. Institutionally, these claims are often made by the state, but they can also be made by the economy or any other public, in the Deweyan sense, that uses its position as a platform to promote its interests over others. Federated disestablishment achieves the aim of mitigating coercive control by creating a functional voice for every interested party in the decision making of education, while also limiting the scope of authority of any one group by enforcing parameters on each voice. In consequence, clear layers of authority with clearly defined scope render explicit the influence they have over us as individuals and in doing so places each authority into conversation with one another.

However, the federated disestablishment of education and state is just one half of the answer that is offered in this book. On its own, it is insufficient, but alongside a suitable interactional design, the Critical Citizen can be realised. In Chapter 7, I argue that the interactional structure of education that is best suited for the realisation of the Critical Citizen is one of internally democratic schooling which employs a Freirean problem-posing pedagogy. I argue that internally democratic problem-posing education mitigates the coercive aspects of one's social environment by creating a schooling environment which enfranchises the pupils and encourages the development of the person through dialogue with one's peers. Furthermore, I argue that through the practice of a problem-posing model of education within the framework of internally democratic schools, pupils are best placed to develop the skills needed to meaningfully participate in society once they leave school because they have developed those skills through experiment and practice within their school environment. Furthermore, in this space and through this pedagogical method, values and beliefs are established by participatory pupils in conversation with the world rather than in competition with the world.

Conclusion

Over the course of the book, I hope to have drawn out the tension between the individual and society in different key politico-educational theories that aim at the resolution to this tension and which inform the model and method of the argument that I have developed. This will be done by identifying the problem of authority as the core to this tension. I hope to have also drawn out the tension in a variety of different ways, and to have done so at the interactional and the institutional levels, and go on to argue that any attempt to resolve the tension between the individual and society, to be coherent and practicable, must aim to resolve the tension at both these levels. I hope to have drawn out the tension within the concept of the citizen itself and within citizenship education as a practice. In response to these problems, I argue that federated disestablishment of education and state and internally democratic problem-posing schooling are capable of offering a coherent resolution to the tension between the individual and society and the realisation of the Critical Citizen. They do this because together they address the coercive force of one's social environment in two meaningful ways. First, they mitigate potentially freedom-constraining aspects of society through the removal of unjustifiable power relations. Second, they render explicit the tension that remains in one's social environment and relationships with others, thereby negating the insidiousness that often accompanies the tension between the individual and society.

References

Advisory Group on Citizenship, 'Education for Citizenship and the Teaching of Democracy in Schools' or The Crick Report. 1998. Qualifications and Curriculum Authority.

Select Committee on Citizenship and Civic Engagement, 'The Ties That Bind: Citizenship and Civic Engagement in the 21st Century' or The Ties That Bind. 2018.

Wilcock, Neil. 2020. 'The Incoherence of the Interactional and Institutional Within Freire's Politico-Educational Project'. *Studies in Philosophy and Education* 39 (4): 399–414.

Wilcock, Neil. 2021. 'Rousseau, Dewey, and Freire: A Political and Educational Method'. *Metaphilosophy*, April, meta.12483.

Chapter 1

Political methodology

Introduction

In this book, I discredit our persistent conceptions of authority and our relationships with it, whether that be with other people or with regard to the institutions of the society we live in. On the back of this destructive aim, I then build an argument in favour of the federated disestablishment of education and state and internally democratic schooling. Later chapters will set out exactly what that means, but I make these arguments on the foundation of a particular approach to political philosophy that shifts away from the orthodox and towards a political philosophy with education and educational theory as the cornerstone of both the means and ends of all that I say. In this way, I believe that we can answer the most troubling problems that stem from the tension between the individual and society, namely the problem of authority. In this preliminary chapter, I shall briefly establish the approach that I shall employ and introduce the key thinkers behind this approach to political philosophy.

There is a strong history of education within political philosophy from Plato's *Republic* to the liberalism of John Locke and beyond. I frame and defend the method that I employ, however, by focussing on three figures that I believe stand out as defenders and practitioners of an educational approach to political philosophy: Jean-Jacques Rousseau, John Dewey, and Paulo Freire. I do so because I believe there is something unique that Rousseau does that stands him apart from those that came before him, and it is through those that follow in his footsteps that I sketch an approach to political philosophy that forms the foundation of my positive thesis.[1]

It is important to note that it need not be the case that the philosophies of Rousseau, Dewey, and Freire are coherent with one another. I neither wish to make the strong claim that they are part of a continuing narrative that is explicit, intentional, and compatible, nor do I wish to cherry-pick bits of their respective politico-educational projects and mash them together into some philosophical Frankenstein. The claim that I do wish to make is that

DOI: 10.4324/9781003271871-2

Rousseau, Dewey, and Freire each develop politico-educational projects that are genealogical and intergenerational in their method; that each of them – to a greater or lesser degree – saw the value of the application of ideas in the world in the development of their theoretical work; that each employed their theory and practice as a method for the development of both the individual and society; that their respective projects aimed to establish freedom of the individual within cooperative association; and that each develop their political philosophies as models of democratic education. In this book, I shall not seek to defend the positions that I ascribe the triumvirate of Rousseau, Dewey, and Freire because it is not their work that is to take centre stage but the positive thesis that I intend to defend. Therefore, I shall only offer my interpretative analysis of their works in order to situate my larger study.

The role and method of Jean-Jacques Rousseau

It seems clear to me that in his core political writings, Rousseau developed a model of education that lies at the foundation of his political project as a whole. There are two initial assumptions that I make. First, that the *First* and *Second Discourse*, *The Social Contract*, and *Émile* represent Rousseau's primary works in political philosophy; this position is supported by Neuhouser (2010), Dent (2005), and Cassirer (1963). The second assumption that I make is that these four works can be read as a complementary and coherent whole. It is a matter of some contention whether this is the case or not. John Charvet argues that Rousseau's political project proves to be incoherent and incompatible with itself (Charvet 2009); Judith Shklar argues that Rousseau presents two intentionally incompatible fictions within his political work (Shklar 1985); Cassirer (1963), however, persuasively argues otherwise. Following Cassirer, Neuhouser (2010, 2012, 2014) also argues that Rousseau's political project is a coherent unified whole. In this, I side with Cassirer and Neuhouser. However, unlike Cassirer and Neuhouser, I place special significance on the role that education plays within this political project.

In two works published in the same year – *Émile* and *The Social Contract* – Rousseau seeks to answer the problems that he identifies in the *First* and *Second Discourse*. The *First Discourse* warns of the dangers of the arts and sciences in corrupting the human animal and *Second Discourse* extends the scope of this narrative to lay at the feet of contemporary society the accusation of coercion and corruption, leaving behind the denatured "Social man". *Émile* and *The Social Contract* seek to reverse that story. In *The Social Contract*, Rousseau takes people as they are, meaning in their corrupted form, and seeks to generate a different cooperative society. In *Émile*, similarly, Rousseau begins in corrupted society but attempts to side-step its effects.

The focus of *Émile* is on the creation of a free individual through education, although it must be noted that there is a clear and intentional misogyny in Rousseau's arguments. Therefore, if his philosophy still has value, then we must consider both the education of Émile as a young man and the distinct education provided to his female counterpart *Sophie* because it is together that they make a unified whole. *Émile* and *The Social Contract* present two stories that address the corruption of the human animal in cooperative association, and it is only when they are read together that Rousseau's political project can be fully understood.

In *Émile*, the reader is presented with a theory of how to overcome the corruption of the individual by the coercive state, educate them to be strong enough to withstand that corruption as an adult, and view society and its problems through a critical gaze. In *The Social Contract*, one follows the human animal's transition from the state of nature to its establishment of a democratic and just society. Rousseau designs the structure of this society in order to minimise the risk of institutions becoming corrupt or arresting the development of egalitarian *amour-propre*, a form of self-love which is felt through one's perception of how they are seen by others – it is a relational form of self-love. Therefore, in *Émile* and *The Social Contract*, we can see a project of freedom being addressed: the former that protects the individual from external coercion by focussing on the individual and the latter by focussing on the institutional structure of society. If we do resemble the animal that Rousseau uncovers primarily in the *First* and *Second Discourse*, then without both arms of this project, the individual and the societal, it is doubtful that any human animal could withstand the inflammation of *amour-propre* and the further corruption of the society in which they live. This might offer an explanation of the tragic life lived by Émile and Sophie in the unfinished sequel of their adventure, *Émile and Sophie; Or, The Solitaries* (*CWR Vol. 13, 685-721*).[2]

Émile is the primary source of Rousseau's answer to what I refer to as the interactional tension between the individual and society. It is a pedagogical novel that tells of the raising of a child under the direction of Jean-Jacques, his tutor and guardian. The aim of the education that Émile receives at the hands of Jean-Jacques is a freedom realised through the acquisition and development of a virtuous character through a radical education, this is then nurtured and sustained through the mutually dependent union with the virtuous Sophie.

In contrast to the interactional model of *Émile* is the response to the tension between the individual and society largely found in the *Social Contract*. This is what I refer to as Rousseau's institutional response to the tension between the individual and society. Here, Rousseau provides an account of the citizen. His aim is to establish a "legitimate and reliable rule of administration" developed for people in their corrupted form (*OC III, 351; CWR Vol. 4, 131*). The concern is that the collective strength found in the formation of society by social contract will undermine the individual's freedom and strength. The social contract therefore must be constructed so as to,

> ... find a form of association that defends and protects the person and goods of each associate with all the common force, and by means of which each one, uniting with all, nevertheless obeys only himself and remains as free as before.
>
> (OC III, 360; CWR Vol. 4, 138)

The realisation of the society that Rousseau describes in *The Social Contract* is a demanding task because it requires the sacrifice of individual freedom and the assumption of responsibilities towards the other members of the newly formed social contract. The individual must cede the authority of the individual in order to join in union with others. This union is a society of equals because each individual gains their share of the rights alienated by the other members of the union and therefore gains as much as they lose. Rousseau expresses the terms of this social contract in the following way, "*Each of us puts his person and all his power in common under the supreme direction of the general will; and in a body we receive each member as an indivisible part of the whole*" (OC III, 361; CWR Vol. 4, 139). As such, a person is both citizen and subject: a participant in the sovereign body and subject to the rules of that body.

The citizen as understood in *The Social Contract* is also a demanding role. It is demanding because it is defined and constructed by the state, and it requires that each individual seek the best for society rather than what they perceive to be in their own best interests; and it is demanding because it relies on the individuals of society to equate what is best for society with that which is best for themselves as individuals, and to perceive that judgement clearly and without private bias. While it is demanding, the freedom in a cooperative society structured in the manner defended by Rousseau is understood as being of a greater quality than that of the state of nature, and so, while there may be less freedom in terms of quantity, the citizenry of a republic retains as much freedom as held before its formation. This freedom, however, is incomplete without what Émile contributes to the political project.

The model of freedom developed in *Émile* is a virtue account of freedom. The virtues that Rousseau identifies for Émile are a good judge of character, strong, hardy, humble, an appreciation of the value of knowledge and the authority of one's masters, and a clear understanding of one's proper rank amongst "men" – one of equality. In Rousseau's own words, Émile is described at the age of reason as, "bubbling, lively, animated, without gnawing cares, without long and painful foresight, whole in his present being, and enjoying a fullness in life which seems to want to extend itself beyond him" (OC IV, 419;

CWR Vol. 13, 302). In Book IV of *Émile*, Rousseau describes Émile's essential character again. He writes,

> Émile possesses a tender and sensitive soul, but he values nothing according to the price set by opinion; thus, although he likes to please others, he will care little about being esteemed by them. From this it follows that he will be more affectionate than polite, that he will never put on airs or make a display, and that he will be more touched by a caress than by a thousand praises. For the same reason he will neglect neither his manners nor his bearing. He may even take some care with his dress, not in order to appear to be a man of taste but to make his looks more agreeable. He will not resort to the gilded frame, and his clothing will never be stained by the mark of riches.
> (*OC IV*, 619; *CWR Vol. 13*, 509–10)

These virtues are learnt through education and the guidance of the tutor Jean-Jacques. Rousseau describes the character of Émile often (*OC IV*, 418–25; *CWR Vol. 13*, 302–7, and *OC IV*, 669–71; *CWR Vol. 13*, 509–11) but often overlooked is the corresponding character of Sophie. Without the union of Émile and Sophie, neither are complete and therefore it is important to draw a picture of the working unit of the human animal. Unfortunately, the qualities that Rousseau gives to Sophie are problematic and serve less to define an integral member of a union between the monogamous and heterosexual partners, and more to highlight the shortcomings of man as Rousseau understands him. Sophie exists to please her man, and she does so with a set of qualities that are framed as manipulations and tools of control – nothing that serves her as an independent individual. There is nothing in Sophie that I can see as a quality that ought to be encouraged and imported into the character of Émile. Instead, it seems more accurate to suggest that Émile's character and the character of man, as Rousseau frames it, is inadequate for the flourishing of woman in society.

Rousseau is guilty of ascribing to women responsibility for moral failures and sexual impulses in men. He does this often and uses it as a premise in many arguments to justify and explain the necessity of the different roles that men and women ought to have in society. One example of this is when he writes,

> Is it our fault that they please us when they are pretty, that their mincing ways seduce us, that the art which they learn from you attracts us and please us, that we like to see them tastefully dressed, that we let them sharpen at their leisure the weapons with which they subjugate us?
> (*OC IV*, 701; *CWR Vol. 13*, 538)

It is in virtue of Rousseau's corrupted and prejudiced view of women that the virtues he ascribes to Sophie are coquetry and modesty; in addition, she must be gentle, chaste, decent, passive, weak, subservient, timid, and patient. Sophie also represents Rousseau's idea of the Spartan woman – a person that he paints as strong and controlling in their own way, in ways that limited the excesses of men and directed them better than they could do without guidance, and without stepping on their fragile egos. He writes,

> You will cause a nobler ambition to be born in them—that of reigning over great and strong souls, the ambition of the women of Sparta, which was to command men. A bold, brazen, scheming woman who knows how to attract her lovers only by coquetry and to keep them only by favours makes them obey her like valets in servile and common things; however, in the woman who is at once decent, lovable, and self-controlled, who forces those about her to respect her, who has reserve and modesty, who, in a word, sustains love by means of esteem, sends her lovers with a nod to the end of the world, to combat, to glory, to death, to anything she pleases. This seems to me to be a nobler empire, and one well worth the price of its purchase.
>
> (OC IV, 745; CWR Vol. 13, 573)

In order to save Rousseau from the hole that he has dug himself, it is necessary to engage in a little critical reconstruction. Despite Rousseau asserting to the contrary, bringing the genders together in their education, respecting them as equals in that education, and modifying the education of Émile to address the oppression of women seem to be wholly in the spirit of Rousseau's politico-educational project. Teach all as Émile is taught but teach them also their correct place in a society, which includes women in the public sphere, teach the balance and responsibilities of both the private and public spheres, ensure that women are not held up merely as ornaments and objects of sexual gratification, and then, Émile and Sophie can enter civil society as equals. It feels at times redundant to make an argument such as this, but it would be naïve to suggest that some of the arguments that Rousseau employs against woman do not continue to hold sway in some circles to this day, and so, equally it feels an important aside and clarification that must be made.

Rousseau has a problem with women, but it is at heart a shameful prejudice which can neither be justified nor forgiven. It is a cause of continual disappointment that Rousseau failed to perceive his own transgression of the shortcomings he unerringly saw in others. The qualities that Rousseau ascribes to women are obviously informed by a limited and biased observation. Furthermore, these qualities are undeniably social not natural, taught and not innate, and even when they are an accurate portrayal of an individual, they are realised often as a consequence of an existing prejudice in society that promotes them and identifies them through confirmation bias. This is particularly disappointing in Rousseau because of the *First* and *Second Discourse* which establish a foundation of philosophical investigation that aims to see beyond the social animal and critiques those who assume that certain qualities in the human animal are natural in order to support their political views.

I bring *Émile* and *The Social Contract* together by emphasising the educative elements of Rousseau's political theory – I call this the centrality of education thesis. I defend the centrality of education thesis by drawing attention to two aspects of Rousseau's political theory. First, to Rousseau's use of fictional devices in his political theory, in particular the tutor Jean-Jacques in *Émile* and the Lawgiver in *The Social Contract*. Rousseau uses these necessary fictions as theoretical tools for the development of his arguments, and they serve two purposes. The first to show where the theory could go if such things existed, and the second to highlight that the perceived end of the political project cannot be reached without a character such as those, and therefore, it cannot be realised in a single generation.

The role of the fictions that Rousseau employs is primarily educative. This is clearly the case within the pages of *Émile*, where the tutor is assumed – a "marvel found" – and operates as a heuristic device. However, education is equally essential within *The Social Contract*. Both Tzvetan Todorov (2001) and John Charvet (2009) see the role of education in *The Social Contract*. Charvet believes that the solution offered is done so through public education, as opposed to the domestic education developed in *Émile* (Charvet 2009, 26). This thought is shared by Todorov who perceives the necessity of public or civic education for the stability of the Republic (Todorov 2001, 26). Rousseau makes it clear that the people, when establishing cooperative association from the state of nature, are not capable of framing good laws or of consistently perceiving the public good, and therefore, they cannot be trusted to express the General Will consistently. The General Will can be broadly understood as the result of a citizen's properly directed reasoning and desire (*OC III*, 371; *CWR Vol. 4*, 147). In light of this, Rousseau introduces the authority of God through the Lawgiver, a character not of the Sovereign and who sits above the Sovereign. This is done in order to guide the Sovereign, which is the collective of the citizens of Rousseau's cooperative association, and ensure that the mandates of the General Will are followed. This is not intended to remain the case, however.

The force of the General Will is educative. The people that join in union do not remain as they were in the state of nature. If the changes that occur to these people are to be positive and lead towards freedom and equality, then the structure and institutions of their union must direct them to be so. Therefore, the Lawgiver plays a similar role as the tutor. They are both, the tutor and the Lawgiver alike, designed to prevent and assist in the reversal of the corruption and coercion of the human animal, while also creating the space for the development of those virtues that sustain and flourish. The Lawgiver is educative. This education takes place over the course of a person's life and from generation to generation until the Lawgiver and the tutor are no longer needed.

The second aspect of Rousseau's political theory that supports the centrality of education thesis is the fact that Rousseau is aware of his fallibility and builds that capacity for error into his political project. He makes it clear that he understands himself as a member of a corrupt society and that he is an example of "Social man". This claim is contentious because Rousseau is often perceived as an arrogant person and therefore can be read as displaying false modesty. Furthermore, it is no doubt true that Rousseau thought almost everyone was more corrupt than himself but he was too clearly aware of the connotations of his own philosophical assumptions, for it to be justified in us dismissing his pronouncements of fallibility (Strauss 1947, 463).

One example of Rousseau's self-awareness is when he writes in the *Second Discourse*, "Everything that comes from Nature will be true; there will be nothing false except what I have involuntarily put in of my own" (*OC III*, 133; *CWR Vol. 3*, 19). Another example is in a reply to a critic of the *Second Discourse*, "Letter by J. J. Rousseau to M. Philopolis", in which Rousseau writes, "I feel too strongly in my own particular case how little I can forego living with men as corrupt as myself, and the wise man himself, if there is one, would not now seek happiness deep in the wilderness" (*OC III*, 235; *Vol. 3*, 131). This fallibility is also apparent in the invention of the literary tools such as the Lawgiver and the tutor Jean-Jacques.

If we understand a consciously fallible Rousseau within his political theory, then it is possible to recast our understanding of that political theory as built upon a foundation of a reflective methodology rather than the expression of a fixed objective belief. Therefore, I claim that Rousseau presents a form of reflective critique with the expectation that his theory will be analysed and refined over the course of time by others.

Together, Rousseau's fallibility and the literary fictions represent the stepping off point from the political project as stated within Rousseau's texts and into the application of that project through the methodology that these tools present. What I mean by this is that the stability of thought that these creations offer and the doubt sewn into Rousseau's thesis ensure that a fixed conclusion is not discoverable within Rousseau's political theory. Instead, we must understand it as subject to evolution and educative in nature.

Although there is much value in Rousseau's politico-educational project, it is not the end of the discussion but merely the opening salvo in the development of a methodological approach to political philosophy with education at the centre. There are significant shortcomings in Rousseau's political project that must be noted. The two most damaging are first, that in virtue of his use of fictional devices there is no possible practical realisation of his political theory because the tools needed to achieve the ends defended are imagined. Therefore, *The Social Contract* and *Émile* should be understood as strictly theoretical works and that they are so is evidenced by the changes made to his theory in the compositions of *On the Government of Poland* (*OC III*, 953-1041; *CWR Vol. 11*, 167–240) and *Constitutional Project for Corsica*

(*OC III*, 901–950; *CWR Vol. 11*, 123–166), which were designed to be used in actual political practice.

The second, and most damaging, shortcoming is that the reflective methodology suggested at parts throughout Rousseau's philosophy is not fully formed and undermined by his active misogyny. As I noted above, Émile's education is the education of a man. The education of women is separate and distinct. In Rousseau's eyes, a woman is to be educated as a wife and companion of a man, not as a citizen and not as a free individual themselves. Rousseau argued in favour of supporting and maintaining the differences perceived within both the public and private spheres – thereby disenfranchising women both in society and at home. The qualities that Rousseau associates exclusively to a particular gender are used to justify this asymmetry and is therefore a huge failure of Rousseau's reflections upon natural character and of his proto-reflective method.

The reflective methodology is further undermined by his insidious teaching habits. In order to control the environment of Émile, Rousseau advocates many tricks and deceits, not least getting him lost in the forest (OC IV, 447–451; CWR Vol. 13, 326–329), forcing him to sleep in a room with a broken window (OC IV, 333–335; CWR Vol. 13, 234–234), and embarrassing him in front of a travelling magician (OC IV, 437–441; CWR Vol. 13, 318–321). In spite of this, Rousseau lays the foundation for a methodological approach to political philosophy that employs education as its animating force and therefore allows for the development of truth over time. To fully realise this method, it is important to introduce the other protagonists to this narrative: John Dewey and Paulo Freire.

The role and method of John Dewey

Dewey is a member of the American pragmatist tradition. As a pragmatist, Dewey was committed to developing knowledge through communal enquiry that began from our current understanding of the world, not from *a priori* propositions. In virtue of this, Dewey did not confine himself to academic work but sought to complement his theory through direct practice. The best example of this is in the establishment of the Laboratory School at the University of Chicago under his direct leadership from 1896 to 1903 (Mayhew and Edwards 2007). It was here as well as in his philosophy that Dewey sought to develop a politicised model of education that aimed to strengthen democracy.

In his pragmatic method, Dewey extended the original scope of enquiry as envisaged by C. S. Peirce, beyond the physical sciences and applied it to the social and moral spheres also. To fully understand this approach to enquiry, it is important to understand Dewey's conception of truth and his treatment of the relationship of means and ends. In short, Dewey believed that truth is that which results from socially shared enquiry and that essences are constructed by the community of enquirers who share the ensuing beliefs. What this means is that truth is not a fixed universal or absolute but a discoverable and reasonably stable belief that is subject to revision as the conditions of enquiry shift. It is more accurately identified as "warranted assertibility" rather than truth (Nissen 1965, 203–10). It is dependent upon its conditions and changes according to those conditions (Dewey 2008b, 10–41; Garrison 1994, 7; Sleeper 2001, 3).

Dewey's understanding of truth is indicative of his delicate understanding of the relationship between means and ends that his pragmatism is structured upon, which is a discussion about the method by which we justify our desired end state of affairs and the process by which we reach that state of affairs. It is Dewey's formulation of the relationship between means and ends that is the part of his methodological approach that I wish to emphasise, and to which I shall continue to return throughout the remainder of this book. It is his conceptualisation of means and ends that we can learn the most from when seeking a philosophical foundation on which to build an alternative political method. Leonard J. Waks, in particular, recognises the importance of means and ends within Dewey's work. He writes, "John Dewey's celebrated analysis of means-ends as a 'continuum' runs through his mature work like a skeletal frame upon which various limbs – valuation, art, technique, science, and democracy – are hinged" (1999, 595). Means and ends also play an important role in Deweyan ethics. Alphonso J. Damico writes, "Men's efforts to resolve moral problems are aided greatly by knowledge of the interconnectedness among social forces and by careful consideration of the relationship between means and ends" (1978, 26).

According to Dewey, one must understand ends, not as final and complete, but as means to further ends. Much like how effects are built upon within the realm of the sciences to create new knowledge and confirm hypotheses. To view ends conventionally – as beyond action – is a mistake. In doing so, in having a fixed end to which we should direct action, our morality becomes bound almost entirely to this end-in-itself and divorces action from the means employed to achieve said aim.

Dewey distinguishes between an end-in-itself and an end-in-view which is synonymous with an "aim". An end-it-itself is a fixed end that is beyond action, whereas ends-in-view are foreseen consequences which are formulated to provide meaning and to direct further action. They are not, according to Dewey, ends of action. "In being ends of *deliberation* they are redirecting pivots *in* action" (Dewey 2008b, 156). A person formulates an aim by first formulating a wish, "an emotional reaction against the present state of things and a hope for something different" (Dewey 2008b, 161). However, this wish exists only in the context of the present state of affairs, "it is a romantic embellishment of the present… Its natural home is not in the future but in the dim past or in some distant and supposedly better part of the present world" (Dewey 2008b, 161). Only when this wish is calculated through the means for its realisation does it become an aim.

Ends-in-view are therefore intimately connected with the means, and the means too are subject to Deweyan analysis. According to Dewey, one must understand means, not as self-justifying or as justified beyond doubt, but within the context of the consequences that they produce. As such, means are subject to revision and while many may be relatively stable, nothing is fixed and static. The means employed, therefore, must be justified by the end-in-view and re-evaluated as that end-in-view shifts over time. The relationship between the means and the ends is not fully explained by this unilateral position. If means and ends are to be understood as truly interconnected, then the ends-in-view must be justified by the means employed also. Therefore, the question of the relationship between means and ends is central to any consistent understanding of Dewey's politico-educational project, and once highlighted is perceivable throughout Dewey's philosophical thought.

Karuna Mantena argues that while Dewey believed that means and ends were deeply interdependent, "the only way means could be justified was by reference to the end toward which they aim" (2012, 13). According to Mantena, this was central to Dewey's pragmatic method in which ends-in-view are adjusted, "in light of objective consequential effects" (2012, 13). The consequence of this view though, according to Mantena, was that Dewey's theory of means–ends was, in some sense, committed to an "overly objective instrumentalism" (2012, 13). It disassociated the particular agent from the particular act so that as long as the morally relevant act was performed it did not matter who performed that action. By distancing the actor and the acted upon from the act itself, Dewey's theory of means–ends thereby misses the subjective relevance. Mantena writes,

> … from the standpoint of enlightened instrumentalism, if the act is taken to be correct in that it is properly directed toward achieving its end, there is little worry about the ways in which the actor is affected (changed or compromised) by the act itself.
>
> (2012, 13–14)

However, Mantena dismisses Dewey's conceptualisation of means and ends too quickly and limits her interpretation by only referencing one essay – "Means and Ends: Their Interdependence" (Dewey 1991). Mantena does not draw upon any work in which Dewey formulated a positive analysis of means and ends, only this short essay which is a response to Leon Trotsky's, *Their Morals and Ours* (1968). Dewey avoids sacrificing agent subjectivity by drawing a distinction between primary and secondary dimensions of experience. This distinction, according to Waks, is at the centre of Dewey's conception of means and ends. Primary experiences are those direct interactions with the world that lead to the formation of beliefs. "For Dewey, life activities undergirded by adequate habit and intelligence-in-action constitute primary experience" (Waks 1999, 598). This is contrasted with secondary dimension of experience which occurs when the beliefs acquired through primary experience are frustrated. It is "characterised by reflective delay" (Waks 1999, 598). A re-analysis occurs though a sharper and more attentive focus on the relative causal relations. In Waks' words, "Enquiry leads to re-cognition" (1999, 598).

Enquiry, for Dewey, is the same as it was for Peirce, and it should be understood as a reconstructive process following the frustration of a previously held belief that leads to a new belief. As such, it is clear that an end-in-view exists as an object of the secondary dimension of experience. Ends-in-view, according to Waks' understanding, "are framed in and are intelligible only within unsettled situations" (Waks 1999, 599). The primary dimension of experience is restored once an end-in-view and the means to achieve it have been selected and then acted out. Therefore, the end result must be understood as the "qualitative whole of primary experience, and not as a *part* broken off to guide the taking of means" (Waks 1999, 600). An end is both the means taken that led to it coming to be and the experience itself. It is what Waks calls a "cumulative gestalt" (1999, 600). This is in contrast to an end-in-view that is merely a calculation or predicted outcome from within secondary experience.

In unpacking the distinction between an end result and an end-in-view in this way, Waks is able to show, not just that the two concepts are distinct, but that they are incomparable. One cannot compare an end-in-view, which are the objects of desire, and end results. They do not differ in degree or amount, they are located in the different dimensions of experience, one primary and the other secondary, and as a result, "the object thought of and the outcome *never* agree" (Dewey 2008c, 173). To try and understand an ending in primary experience as comparable with that devised in secondary experience is therefore a category mistake because no matter how many variables are considered and analysed when devising an end-in-view, that idea that exists only in secondary experience can never adequately characterise the result from the means taken. Waks writes,

> ... that situation remains fluid and indefinite unless and until, in its qualitative totality, it calls for more focused and discriminating attention. That would entail an *additional* shift to the secondary dimension of experience at the close of the primary phase.
>
> (1999, 601)

However, in that shift one shows that the end is not a termini of action because it represents a new beginning and it is the new situation and not the end selected earlier to guide action that, "determines the focus of evaluation at that point" (Waks 1999, 601–602). With this clarification as to the meaning of Dewey's relationship between means and ends, it is clear to see the mistake that Mantena has made in her interpretation. The agent is not divorced from the means taken, nor the end-in-view because these things can only be understood as a part of the tension of the individual as a part of their secondary experience. In fact, the means and the ends understood this way are defined by the agent and cannot be understood separately from the agent. Mantena makes a category mistake in attributing to Dewey a belief in an end that is beyond action and therefore separate from the actor.

By following Dewey's pragmatic method, informed by his conceptualisation of means and ends, we can see that, for Dewey there is no end of enquiry or absolute truth, in the Peircean sense, because the social conditions in which we formulate our aims change in response to our actions and demand continual re-analysis and reflection. This is why Dewey's political and educational philosophy is genealogical and intergenerational because it provides a method that determines a model of social enquiry that persists for as long as there is cooperative association.

Dewey places great importance upon education and democracy in his political philosophy. In one of his most significant works, *Democracy and Education*, Dewey endeavours, "to detect and state the ideas implied in a democratic society and to apply these ideas to the problems of the enterprise of education" (2008a, 3). Dewey argues that education is essential because without it society would either fail to form or fail to sustain itself. Without education, the death of one generation would be the death of society; it would be as if the whole of society is wiped out of existence. According to Dewey, there is no growth, there is no development without education (2008a, 4–5).

Through education, Dewey aims to refine and maximise democracy within society as a tool for social change and enfranchisement of the individual. Democracy, when used as a term by Dewey, is more than merely the limited view of democracy as a form of government. Democracy, for Dewey, "is primarily a mode of associated living, of conjoint communicated experience" (2008a, 93). It is, therefore, rule by the people, not solely through elected representatives or the mere act of voting but through participation in a community of enquirers. Education, for Dewey, is not an independent endeavour.

It is the view of Dewey that we develop our understanding of the world through communication with others. It is communication that makes a group of individuals a social group. Without communication, there is no difference between the human animal and parts of a machine. Jim Garrison writes that Dewey's conception of democracy "was less about voting than about equal participation by all in the conversation of humankind. Initiation into this conversation is the purpose of education, and it is the purpose of educational research to provide tools that aid this task" (1994, 13).

This view of communication through social enquiry can be seen in Dewey's writings very early, and it persists throughout his career. Dewey argued that the school, as a part of the community, must be involved in the community. Furthermore, it was Dewey's contention that the students of the school develop the skills and knowledge necessary by direct practice and observation. Therefore, greater interaction between school and society is encouraged. Dewey argues therefore that society cannot exist without education; individuals form a society through communication; and all communication is educative. This process in a societal context is, for Dewey, a form of democracy. Actively engaging in our respective environment through communicative enquiry is the first step to a truly democratic society. This is a preferable model of democracy to a society which is run by the whim of majority and populism.

The role and method of Paulo Freire

Paulo Freire was a revolutionary educational theorist and practitioner who made a name for himself teaching adult literacy to the poor and disenfranchised around the world. The theory behind Freire's literacy programme understood the political world as containing two groups of people, the oppressed and the oppressors. Broadly conceived, the oppressed are those people that, through fear and consent, are "dehumanised" – they become less human – because of the structure and prejudices of the oppressors and of the society to which they both belong. The oppressors are those people who benefit from the existing power structures of society. They need not actively or directly dehumanise another to be an oppressor; they oppress simply in virtue of their privilege. However, according to Freire, this power and the satisfaction of desire do not satisfy the conditions of freedom. Neither the oppressed nor the oppressors are free, they are both enslaved by this inequality. Freire explains this position through the concept of the fear of freedom which he adopts from Erich Fromm (2010).

The fear of freedom is a key inspiration in Freire's psychological analysis of humans caught in oppressive relationships between each other and with the world. For the oppressed, the fear of freedom manifests in two ways: either it creates a barrier to the pursuit of freedom and they thereby remain oppressed or it manifests as a desire to assume the role of the oppressor. Both of these manifestations arise in the mind of the oppressed as a result of their perception of the oppressor as possessing authority over them. In another way, the fear of freedom is found in the psychology of the oppressors because they too are not free. They have been dehumanised by the practice of oppression and hold on to their position of power because they "are afraid of losing their 'freedom' to oppress" (Freire 2017, 20 ftn). The oppressors take for granted their privilege and their power and become effectively blind to the harm they cause through it.

Freire argues that this societal oppression is cemented and perpetuated through the existing education system. According to Freire, the traditional role of the educator is a role that supports the existing structure of society and existing power relations. It is therefore operating as a tool of continued oppression. It does this by treating students as empty containers that are to be filled with knowledge by the teacher – this knowledge is presented as fixed and questions are not encouraged. We can see in this relationship between student and teacher a clear divide between their roles. Freire describes the student–teacher relationship as of being narrative in character. The student is treated as ignorant and expected to remain passive. The teacher assumes a dominant role over the student as a distributor and arbitrator of knowledge. As a result, according to Freire, knowledge becomes soporific rather than empowering. He writes,

> The student records, memorises, and repeats ... Narration (with the teacher as narrator) leads the students to memorise mechanically the narrated content. Worse yet, it turns them into 'containers,' into 'receptacles' to be "filled" by the teacher. The more completely he fills the receptacles, the better a teacher he is. The more meekly the receptacles permit themselves to be filled, the better students they are.
>
> (2017, 58)

Freire calls this the banking method of education, where the teacher deposits information into the minds of students who receive the information without question. Their task being to memorise and repeat. This is unsatisfactory to Freire. For one reason, this method encourages no independent thinking. In fact, it stifles, through its lack, "creativity, transformation, and knowledge" (Freire 2017, 58). For Freire, this divorces the student from enquiry and hinders their ability to comprehend knowledge and to discover new knowledge.

In response to this, Freire aimed to develop an educational theory and practice that could lead to the overcoming of these deeply ingrained oppressor–oppressed relationships and, in turn, to the emancipation of all people. It is this revolutionary pedagogy, which Freire practised working primarily with the illiterate and the poor across the world, most notably in Brazil, Chile, and Africa (Irwin 2012, 8; Schugurensky 2014, 43), as well as his problematisation of didactic knowledge transference, that I wish to highlight as Freire's key contribution to my methodological construction. It is in the relationships between people and their cooperation in the development of a collective of critically questioning individuals that Freire contributes to the politico-educational dialogue that forms the foundation of my enquiry.

In *Pedagogy of the Oppressed*, Freire argues that the vocation of the human animal is "humanisation" and provides a theoretical and practical methodology for overcoming the corrupting and coercive state of affairs that persists. This is not euphemistic language but terminology which at once shows Freire's Catholic heritage, believing as he does that humans have become less human as a consequence of our corruption, but also his Marxism because he places the source of that dehumanisation in the structure of society rather than within the human animal. Humanisation is a technical term of Freire's which means to become "more fully human" and it acts as his normative goal (Freire 2017, 18). To become more fully human, one is becoming less oppressed, and in being oppressed, one is dehumanised.

Freire proposes what he calls problem-posing education as the educational method to provide the foundation by which we can overcome our corruption and dehumanisation. Problem-posing education understands knowledge, not as a set of facts or values to be remembered but as a consequence of communal enquiry. "Knowledge" Freire writes, "emerges only through invention and re-invention, through the restless, impatient, continuing, hopeful enquiry human beings pursue in the world, with the world, and with each other" (2017, 45). It emerges through the enquiry of peers with each other, the results of which are understood as fluid and revisable.

It is through dialogue that the students both learn and teach. It is through dialogue that the teacher both learns and teaches. Freire writes, "Problem-posing education affirms men and women as beings in the process of *becoming*— as unfinished, uncomplicated beings in and with a likewise unfinished reality" (2017, 57). Freire states that we are aware of this unfinished status, and this state motivates the learner to continue their enquiry and understand education as an ongoing activity. Problems are discussed, debated, and challenged, and from these initial presented stimuli, new problems arise that are, themselves, discussed, debated, and challenged.

Problem-posing education is therefore a dialectical process that is facilitated by the educators who use their skills to assist learners in, first seeing their oppression, then exploring that through the learners' own understanding of the world. Conclusions drawn and inference made from this process are then fed back in as problems to be addressed through dialogue with their peers and their community. Wayne Au, an advocate of Freirean pedagogy, describes problem-posing education as a process for students and teachers to engage in by, "asking critical questions of the world in which they live, asking questions of the material realities both experience on a day-to-day basis, and critically reflecting on what actions they may take to change those material conditions" (2009, 222).

Similar to Dewey's political enquiry, for Freire, there is not an end to education. He writes, "Education is thus constantly remade in the praxis. In order to be, it must become. Its 'duration' is found in the interplay of the opposites permanence and change" (Freire 2017, 57). Furthermore, it is through this dialogue that human consciousness is developed because it cultivates an environment of reflection of a person's particular reality. The process of becoming conscious in a meaningful way is what Freire calls conscientização (Freire 2017, 41). It is important to note here that the process of conscientização should not be understood as a process of consciousness-raising with a final end in mind, a person has not come to the end of their journey upon reaching critical consciousness because they do not participate absolutely or exclusively in this mode of consciousness. Peter Roberts writes that conscientização is an "ever-evolving process" in continual interaction with a changing world (1996, 186).

An education conducted in this manner is designed to be emancipatory and enfranchising, but, according to Freire, to be so, it must do more than bring freedom. A pedagogy of the oppressed must be such that the oppressed themselves are direct participants in its practice and design. There are two things that are being argued for in Freire's problem-posing education which are seen as intimately connected; there is emancipation from oppression, and there is the development of the individual. The former is achieved through the latter, and this leads to people challenging the oppressive aspects of their world. Freire's resolution to the contradiction between the individual and the world is to empower the individual through a dialogical educational model. It is through the word that we transform the world.

Rousseau, Dewey, and Freire together

Rousseau, Dewey, and Freire are significant as individuals who have each come to dominate discussions in both political and educational contexts. They are not alone in possessing this quality. Plato, Thomas Hobbes, and John Locke are obvious examples of others who have developed political theses with an educative heart, but Rousseau, Dewey, and Freire stand out as individuals who have approached political philosophy in a particular way. It seems to me that their respective works seek not to use education to shape the human animal to a model of political association, nor are their attempts to frame a model of political association around a specified set of qualities, rights, or responsibilities that are either imposed on the human animal or supposed to be natural to the human animal. Instead, Rousseau, Dewey, and Freire, each and in their own way, present political association and the individual as both subject to continual investigation and reformulation – it is in this way that education is central to their political philosophy.

For such prominent figures as Rousseau, Dewey, and Freire, I find it surprising that so little has been written on their potential overlaps. This surprise is sharpened when one delves a little deeper. I put this oversight on several factors. First, that Dewey's own interpretation and response to Rousseau found especially in his *Democratic Education* expounds a common but mistaken interpretation of Rousseau's *Émile* (Dewey 2008a, 118–25). Second, on the relative failure to acknowledge the influence that Dewey had on, in particular the early thought of, Freire and the focus instead on the influence of Marx, Catholicism, and Critical Theory (Giroux 2017; Elias 1994; Irwin 2012, 8). Lastly, the relative quiet between the philosophical and the educational academic disciplines has led to an ever-widening separation in research and cleaving of the knowledge of education from philosophical thought in each of these respective thinkers and vice versa.

It does not require a great depth of research to see the similarity in the overriding projects of Rousseau, Dewey, and Freire. For each, their model of education and their political projects are mutually interdependent and they stand or fall together; they each employ a model of education that is designed to provide the pedagogical insight and space for the flourishing of freedom, in particular a freedom that persists in the face of a corrupting and coercive social environment; and they each employ a political project that is democratic, radical, and built upon a view of the interdependence of theory and practice. Delving a little deeper into this last point, it is important to note that this fealty to democracy is not something to take for granted, because democracy, for each of them, extends far beyond the mere act of voting and representative government but permeates through all aspects of public life and it has its foundations built by education – not to mention the fact that each of them lived through times when democratic governance was either under threat or, in Rousseau's case, at the beginning of its rebirth – and feeding back into the centrality of education within their respective thought, the strength of the democracy envisaged is found through the education of the people.

Most telling, however, is the fact that Rousseau, Dewey, and Freire each, as the aim of their respective politico-educational projects, seek to construct a philosophy which develops individuals into active and engaged citizens without sacrificing their own private interests or at the expense of freedom. This becomes more apparent when one realises that there exists an academic thread through the thought of Rousseau, Dewey, and Freire. A link that connects them and draws them closer together. We can see this clearly in Dewey's analysis of Rousseau in *Democracy and Education* (2008a), and this book should be seen, at least in part, as Dewey's response to Rousseau's *Émile*. Additionally, although rarely noted, Dewey's political philosophy played a significant role in Freire's work. Darcísio Natal Muraro (2013) and Moacir Gadotti (1996) both note the influence that Dewey has had on Freire. Therefore, there is an under-researched and direct chain of influence that deserves exploration.

Conclusion

Rousseau lays the foundation for a distinct methodological approach for political philosophy with education as a central component by constructing a model that aims to develop the individual within society and the institutions of that society through education. Dewey continues with a similar project and argues in favour of breaking down the barriers between the school and the world, urging that the school should be treated as a microcosm of the world, and that the people subject to this education should define the world, rather than the world define them. In doing so, Dewey provides a methodological answer to the limitations of Rousseau's politico-educational project, such as addressing the persistent problem of an authoritative relationship between teacher and student and employing a reflective methodology explicitly and consistently. Building upon pragmatic foundations, Dewey was able to develop a form of progressive education that proved implementable, democratic, and a tool for social change.

The difference between Dewey and Rousseau is largely one of attitude towards the powerful influence of society on the individual – Dewey embraces this influence while recognising its destructive potential, whereas Rousseau designs a societal structure and model of education that aims to create the potential for the constructive and positive influence of society because of its otherwise necessarily destructive impact. Freire extends Rousseau's project by perceiving this as a revolutionary process. Unlike Dewey, Freire does not remain optimistic about the levels of social control within people's social environment. Unlike Rousseau, Freire does not succumb to pessimism with regard to our chances of overcoming that social control. Freire moves beyond the work of Rousseau in the belief that the possibility of overcoming the coercion of an oppressive world is very real, not simply a theoretical possibility.

Further to this, Freire differs from both Rousseau and Dewey in adding a truly global perspective as the scope of political consideration. Freire's "world" is distinct from Rousseau's "republic" and Dewey's "publics". Rousseau's society is only the immediate local area, the small republic with limited suffrage. There is no consideration by Rousseau of how this republic affects those beyond its bounds of governance or even the non-citizens within its boundaries. Dewey's publics are groups with which individuals' associate, to which they feel they belong, and whose interests they actively pursue (Allport 1989, 285). There are a multitude of publics, and any one individual will likely be a member of many, with overlapping interests and internal tensions. What is key is that these publics need not apply to any particular geographical area, but as the many publics to which any one individual belongs will be in tension with each other at times, it is not clear how these publics will be able to interact meaningfully with one another.

In contrast, Freire speaks of the world to which we all belong. Problem-posing education transforms not simply how the world is perceived but what the world is. Through his endeavours in educational practice at both the interactional and the institutional levels, Freire provides surer foundations for educational practice than Rousseau and Dewey were able to offer, while maintaining a commitment to ensuring that this practice is informed by the community and the individuals who are learning. These differences do not stand as obstacles to using Rousseau, Dewey, and Freire as the foundation for an approach to political philosophy. In fact, I see these differences as a part of the educative approach that they offer and it is on these foundations that I rest the arguments forthcoming in the subsequent chapters of this book.

Notes

1 I explore the connections between these three writers and the value of reading them together in more detail in my essay, "Rousseau, Dewey, and Freire: A Political and Educational Method" (Wilcock 2021).
2 Throughout this book I shall reference the work of Rousseau according to convention. Therefore, I shall reference his collected works in English by the initialism CWR followed by the volume that the text appears in. When relevant I shall also reference the original French text from the *Œuvres Complètes* edited by Bernard Gagnebin and Marcel Raymond, with the initialism OC followed by the volume number.

References

Allport, Gordon W. 1989. 'Individual and Social Psychology'. In *The Philosophy of John Dewey*, edited by Paul Arthur Schilpp and Lewis Edwin Hahn, 3rd ed., 263–90. The Library of Living Philosophers, Volume 1. La Salle, IL: Open Court.

Au, Wayne. 2009. 'Fighting With the Text: Contextualising and Recontextualising Freire's Critical Pedagogy'. In *The Routledge International Handbook of Critical Education*, edited by Michael W. Apple, 221–31. Routledge International Handbook Series. New York: Routledge.

Cassirer, Ernst. 1963. *The Question of Jean-Jacques Rousseau*. Bloomington: Indiana University Press.

Charvet, John. 2009. *The Social Problem in the Philosophy of Rousseau*. Cambridge: Cambridge University Press.

Damico, Alfonso J. 1978. *Individuality and Community: The Social and Political Thought of John Dewey*. Gainesville: University Presses of Florida.

Dent, N. J. H. 2005. *Rousseau*. Routledge Philosophers. London; New York: Routledge.

Dewey, John. 1991. 'Means and Ends: Their Interdependence'. In *The Later Works of John Dewey, 1925-1953. Vol. 13: 1938–1939*, edited by Jo Ann Boydston, 349–55. Carbondale: Southern Illinois University Press.

Dewey, John. 2008a. 'Democracy and Education'. In *The Middle Works of John Dewey, 1899-1924, Volume 9: 1916*, edited by Jo Ann Boydston, 1–370. Carbondale: Southern Illinois University Press.

Dewey, John. 2008b. 'Experience and Philosophic Method'. In *The Later Works of John Dewey, 1925-1953, Volume 1: 1925*, edited by Jo Ann Boydston, 10–41. Carbondale: Southern Illinois University Press.

Dewey, John. 2008c. 'Human Nature and Conduct'. In *The Middle Works of John Dewey, 1899–1924, Volume 14: 1922*, edited by Jo Ann Boydston, 1–227. Carbondale: Southern Illinois University Press.

Elias, John L. 1994. *Paulo Freire: Pedagogue of Liberation*. Malabar, FL: Krieger Pub. Co.

Freire, Paulo. 2017. *Pedagogy of the Oppressed*. Translated by Myra Bergman Ramos. London: Penguin Books.

Fromm, Erich. 2010. *The Fear of Freedom*. London: Routledge.

Gadotti, Moacir. 1996. 'A voz do biógrafo brasileiro: A prática à altura do sonho'. In *Paulo Freire: uma biobibliografia*, edited by Moacir Gadotti and Ana Maria Araújo Freire, 69–116. São Paulo: Cortez Editora: Instituto Paulo Freire; UNESCO.

Garrison, Jim W. 1994. 'Realism, Deweyan Pragmatism, and Educational Research'. *Educational Researcher* 23 (1): 5–14.

Giroux, Henry. 2017. 'Critical Theory and Educational Practice'. In *The Critical Pedagogy Reader*, edited by Antonia Darder, Rodolfo D. Torres, and Marta Baltodano, 3rd ed., 31–55. New York: Routledge.

Irwin, Jones. 2012. *Paulo Freire's Philosophy of Education: Origins, Developments, Impacts and Legacies*. London: Continuum.

Mantena, Karuna. 2012. 'Gandhi and the Means-Ends Question in Politics'. *Occasional Papers of the School of Social Science, Institute for Advanced Study* 46 (June): 1–25.

Mayhew, Katherine Camp, and Anna Camp Edwards. 2007. *The Dewey School: The Laboratory School of the University of Chicago 1896–1903*. New York, S.l.: Routledge.

Muraro, Darcísio Natal. 2013. 'Relações Entre a Filosofia e a Educação de John Dewey e de Paulo Freire'. *Educação & Realidade* 38 (3): 813–29.

Neuhouser, Frederick. 2010. *Rousseau's Theodicy of Self-Love: Evil, Rationality, and the Drive for Recognition*. Oxford: Oxford University Press.

Neuhouser, Frederick. 2012. 'The Critical Function of Genealogy in the Thought of J.-J. Rousseau'. *The Review of Politics* 74 (03): 371–87.

Neuhouser, Frederick. 2014. *Rousseau's Critique of Inequality: Reconstructing the Second Discourse*. Cambridge: Cambridge University Press.

Nissen, Lowell. 1965. 'Dewey's Theory of Truth'. *The Personalist* 46 (2): 203–10.

Roberts, Peter. 1996. 'Rethinking Conscientisation'. *Journal of Philosophy of Education* 30 (2): 179–96.

Rousseau, Jean-Jacques. 1992. *Discourse on the Origins of Inequality (Second Discourse); Polemics; and, Political Economy*. Edited by Roger D. Masters and Christopher Kelly. The Collected Writings of Rousseau, Vol. 3. Hanover: University Press of New England.

Rousseau, Jean-Jacques. 1994. *Social Contract; Discourse on the Virtue Most Necessary for a Hero; Political Fragments; and, Geneva Manuscript*. Edited by Roger D. Masters, Christopher Kelly, and Judith R. Bush. The Collected Writings of Rousseau, Vol. 4. Hanover: University Press of New England.

Rousseau, Jean-Jacques. 1999. *Émile. Éducation. Morale. Botanique*. Œuvres Complètes, IV. Paris: Gallimard.

Rousseau, Jean-Jacques. 2003. *Du contrat social. Écrits politiques*. Edited by Bernard Gagnebin and François Bouchardy. Œuvres Complètes, III. Paris: Gallimard.

Rousseau, Jean-Jacques. 2005. *The Plan for Perpetual Peace, On the Government of Poland, and Other Writings on History and Politics*. Edited by Christopher Kelly. The Collected Writings of Rousseau, Vol. 11. Hanover: University Press of New England.

Rousseau, Jean-Jacques. 2010a. 'Émile and Sophie; Or, The Solitaries'. In *Emile, or, On Education: Includes Emile and Sophie; Or, The Solitaries*, edited by Christopher Kelly, translated by Allan Bloom. The Collected Writings of Rousseau, Vol. 13. Hanover: University Press of New England.

Rousseau, Jean-Jacques. 2010b. 'Émile'. In *Emile, or, On Education: Includes Émile and Sophie; Or, The Solitaries*. Edited by Christopher Kelly. Translated by Allan Bloom. The Collected Writings of Rousseau, Vol. 13. Hanover: University Press of New England.

Schugurensky, Daniel. 2014. *Paulo Freire*. London; New York: Bloomsbury Academic, an imprint of Bloomsbury Publishing.

Shklar, Judith N. 1985. *Men and Citizens: A Study of Rousseau's Social Theory.* Cambridge Studies in the History and Theory of Politics. London; New York: Cambridge University Press.

Sleeper, R. W. 2001. *The Necessity of Pragmatism: John Dewey's Conception of Philosophy.* Urbana, IL; Chicago, IL: University of Illinois Press.

Strauss, Leo. 1947. 'On the Intention of Rousseau'. *Social Research* 14 (4): 455–87.

Todorov, Tzvetan. 2001. *Frail Happiness: An Essay on Rousseau.* Translated by John T. Scott and Robert D. Zaretsky. University Park: Pennsylvania State University Press.

Trotsky, Leon. 1968. *Their Morals and Ours.* London: New Park Publications.

Waks, Leonard J. 1999. 'The Means-Ends Continuum and the Reconciliation of Science and Art in the Later Works of John Dewey'. *Transactions of the Charles S. Peirce Society* 35 (3): 595–611.

Wilcock, Neil. 2021. 'Rousseau, Dewey, and Freire: A Political and Educational Method'. *Metaphilosophy*, April, meta.12483. https://doi.org/10.1111/meta.12483

Chapter 2

The Critical Citizen

Introduction

In this chapter, I shall focus on one dominant aspect of Rousseau, Dewey, and Freire – a key component that they share with one another and that operates as the aim of their respective educational theory within their politico-educational projects: the development of the person. I shall begin with a brief justification of employing this as an aim of education within the context of a political methodology. Then, I shall draw out the conceptualisation of the person that I defend as this aim by looking in more detail at each component of the person that operates as my aim of education. This political person that I develop is descriptively communitarian, normatively cosmopolitan, an active participant in one's society, and a possessor of both rights and responsibilities. I refer to this person as the Critical Citizen. I employ this term because I believe that it captures the character of the concept. The use of the word 'citizen' may be contentious because it could be seen to imply membership to a state, but this need not be the case. We only need to look at Diogenes the Cynic, who stated, "I am a citizen of the world" (Diogenes Laertius 2018, VI 63) to see that we can understand the citizen outside of a commitment to a particular state or people. And while I would wish to avoid the connotations, I believe that term, especially when coupled with the term 'critical' which does much to balance the implications alluded to, is best placed to serve the function of identifying a sense of societal responsibility alongside the values of individual freedom and the pursuit of social change.

The citizen as an aim of education

The concept of the citizen sits at the centre of our political and educational conversation. It is a demand for rights and representation, but it is also a demanding ideal of embodied values and responsibilities. It is appealed to across the political spectrum, and it can be seen clearly in the new rights claims that have gained traction over the last few decades by diverse groups, many of which have suffered and continue to suffer significant discrimination

DOI: 10.4324/9781003271871-3

and oppression. In recent years, the rights and treatment of women have returned to the public debate as the '#MeToo' and the 'Reclaim these Streets' movements demand a re-evaluation of our embedded social attitudes and treatment of women as sexual objects. We have also seen LGBTQ+ rights gain traction in recent years, and we have seen a significant shift in public attitude and legislation take place. For example, as recently as the 1960s, consensual sex between two adult males was still illegal in the United Kingdom. It is now the case that through human rights and anti-discrimination legislation, people from traditionally oppressed groups are gaining a voice and representation. Homosexual acts were first decriminalised in England and Wales in *The Sexual Offences Act* 1967. Since then, a great number of small steps have taken place and, hopefully, will continue to take place both legislatively and in the minds of the public. Same-sex couples can now apply to adopt children; all sex-specific legislation has been replaced with gender-neutral language; and same-sex marriage, with certain restrictions, was legalised in *The Marriage (Same Sex Couples) Act* 2013. These acts represent but a small number of the positive changes that have taken place in United Kingdom legislation over recent years. However, it would be naïve to think that rights claims are progressively expanding and that public attitudes are becoming progressively more accepting.

Prejudice continues institutionally and in the conscious and unconscious mindsets of individuals. It is embedded in our society, but we are often blind to it, expressing surprise and disgust when explicit expressions are voiced, yet unwilling to challenge our own implicit prejudice or the prejudices supported by the institutional structure of society. A key example of this is the aftershock of the referendum on the United Kingdom leaving the EU, which was effectively reduced to a mudslinging campaign of propaganda and accusations of racism. Another is the recent surge in high-profile cases of racism in professional football and other public arenas, most notably after England's penalty shootout loss in the European Championships final in 2021, which is spoken of by many as if there is a return of racism rather than an emboldened expression of latent racism. The present Government of the United Kingdom is offering the clearest example of continued and abhorrent racism with their introduction and defence of the Illegal Immigration bill, something that I anticipate having received Royal assent by the time this book has been published.

What makes the citizen such a fascinating aim of education is that in contrast to these campaigns for individual rights and their relative success, citizenship and citizenship education are often clearly employed in the name of socially conservative ends as well. In these instances, values are defended that are often nationalistic, patriarchal, heteronormative, or more broadly oppressive. This is just one small aspect of citizenship or political education being used to cultivate a specific and socially conservative set of values. Education has been employed by some as a way of maintaining existing power relations or as a way of returning to an ideal past where control and conformity act as the aims of political education. Tristan McCowan identifies this trend within education. He writes, "It is as common for citizenship education to be justified on the basis of the maintenance of order and control in society, and of legitimization of current political institutions, as on the development of empowered political agents" (McCowan 2009, 4).

The aim is explicitly stated in the recent report by the select committee on citizenship and civic engagement, *The Ties that Bind*, in which it is stated that, "citizenship education, ... should be the first great opportunity for instilling and developing our values, encouraging social cohesion, and creating active citizens" (*The Ties That Bind* 2018, 4). It is an expression of values to be imposed on others in order for them to then embody those values. Examples such as the recitation of the Lord's Prayer in Christian countries, a practice that I remember in my state primary school, or the pledge of allegiance in the United States of America are undeniable and explicit examples of attempts to inculcate specific values and character within young people in this way. The contrast between this and the extension of rights to groups traditionally othered by society is obvious. In the latter case, change is being made in society through the campaigns and civil disobedience of members of the citizenry, whereas in the former the status quo is being reinforced by a prescribed set of values.

The complexity behind the citizen and the aims of citizenship or political education are evident in the developments in the political conception of citizenship and citizenship education in the United Kingdom in recent years. Since the introduction of compulsory citizenship education in England and Wales in 2002, there has followed a confusing mix of policies and curricula. Fundamental British Values (FBV), the Prevent Strategy, the introduction of the National Citizenship Service (NCS), and changes in the national curriculum have introduced a confusion of ideologies and a tension between the intentions of a socially conservative vision being developed at the political level and the professional standards of teachers whose focus is on the individual under their charge and not some ideological political vision. The tension between these two forces is but one instance of the tension between the individual and society that will continue to resurface throughout the course of this book.

It is true that I offer here a reasonably broad account of the rights of a citizen. I do not limit it to the narrower rights to vote, stand for office, and hold those in office accountable. I understand it to include all those characteristics and qualities of a person that inform their ability to access full participation in society as a citizen. This therefore includes those parts of ourselves which others may wish to legislate against. The broader understanding is preferable because it incorporates the citizen as a forensic term alongside the citizen as a holder of rights and bearer of responsibilities.

I am inspired by the efforts for self-determination throughout history but worry about the atomisation of society as we increasingly define ourselves in terms of the individual. The pursuit of individual freedom continues unabated by the progress made and challenges our understandings of things rarely questioned before this period in history. Yet, the pursuit for a freedom beyond the narrow scope of the individual has been boxed in by a capitalist economy. The citizen that I perceive as the aim of education and an answer to the tension between the individual and society will prove to be descriptively communitarian, normatively cosmopolitan, an active participant in one's society, and a possessor of both rights and responsibilities – my very own Émile. In the rest of this chapter, I shall look at each of these components in turn.

Descriptively communitarian

One quality that I perceive as essential for the character of the Critical Citizen is that they are descriptively communitarian. According to the communitarian, political theory must focus on the principles found in the traditions and practices of particular societies because the moral standards of cooperative association differ across communities and there is no single universal standard to which all should be held (MacIntyre 1978; Taylor 1985, 15–57). This is setup in contrast to political theory that champions, or holds implicit, universal moral values.

Further to this, communitarianism places emphasis on a concept of the self that is, at least in part, defined or constituted by various attachments particular to the individual, such as familial ties and religious tradition. These attachments, it is argued, being held so close to the individual, cannot be abstracted from the individual, and as such, the political sphere must extend beyond concerns for conditions of autonomous action and consider additionally the social attachments which contribute to an individual sense of self and identity (Taylor 1989). The values of citizenship, according to the communitarian, are learnt in the particular attachments to which one belongs. It is within these groups that we learn, "values of civility and self-restraint" and "the virtues of mutual obligation" (Kymlicka and Norman 1994, 363). One learns civic virtues within the groups of which one is a part.

This is in contrast to the contractarian tradition of writers such as Locke, Kant, and Rawls who seek universalisable moral rules or political principles that can be used as the foundation of political association. Rawls, of course, takes his participants behind the proverbial curtain and into the Original Position, so that, obscured by the Veil of Ignorance, we are unaware of even our own identifying characteristics when deciding on the principles of justice to govern society (Rawls 1999). This is anathema to the communitarian theorist because it ignores the importance of the particular values of a person's local community (MacIntyre 1978; Taylor 1985). This can be a normative objection to ideal theory or a descriptive objection. It is one thing to note the limitations of ideal theory in developing moral and political principles without considering the particular attitudes, values, and cultures of the world and how they will react differently to the same set of principles. It is another thing entirely to object to ideal theory because we *ought* to be guided morally and political by the attitudes, values, and cultures of our local community.

The communitarian position is unsatisfactory as the foundation for political theory and the development of a citizenry because the values learnt and the scope of these values can be both limited and limiting. Identification with a group within civil society may put one at odds with those outside of the group when interests do not align. Furthermore, the practices within those groups may run contrary to the values firmly held outside of the group. Groups to which one belongs and identifies may prove too insulated from outside influence, and too insular to impact externally to the group. Even if one of those groups is able to influence the larger society, it is not clear that we would want them to.

Nevertheless, communitarian thought draws our attention to something intuitive and persuasive, in that the starting place for our moral and political development surely is our immediate social environment. We learn our early concepts of right and wrong, fair and unfair, and just and unjust from a small sphere of influence: our parents and immediate family, our friends and teachers, and our heroes and villains. And we develop these beliefs in a very specific social and political context. For example, how our schools and societies are organised; how different people are treated within our community; how inequalities between people are tolerated and how they manifest; how great those inequalities are within our community; and our attitudes towards the environment and non-human animals. These realities shape us and shape our views, and many of the moral, political, and cultural beliefs that we develop in our environment are assumed and unquestioned. Or, at the least, these beliefs that guide us obscure our vision for how else things could be and why those alternatives may be preferable.

The communitarian makes a number of normative and descriptive claims. Simon Caney does a good job of drawing these different components out clearly (Caney 1992). According to Caney, the communitarian is committed to three descriptive theses: the embeddedness thesis, the view that persons are embedded in their communities; the social thesis, the view that persons only develop their moral outlook in society; and the cultural options thesis, the view that persons choose their values, virtues, and identity in the context of the social environment to which they belong. This is intuitively accurate in my view and wholly incontestable. It is certainly the case in Dewey's political philosophy where, much like the communitarian, Dewey argues that our starting place for enquiry must be from our current set of beliefs and norms. This is a fundamental criterion of Dewey's pragmatism because enquiry begins with direct experience. According to Dewey, a person cannot act in a vacuum – that their actions and their beliefs are informed by their social environment. It is because a person cannot be abstracted from society that

Dewey uses, as the foundation for political and social enquiry, our existing moral, political, and cultural viewpoints.

Similarly, the foundation of Freire's pedagogical practice is built on existing knowledge and belief structures. Freire speaks of the human animal's dehumanisation as a "historical reality" (Freire 2017, 17). It is something that we have suffered and continue to suffer as a result of living in a society structurally supported by oppression. The inverse, humanisation, is "constantly negated," through injustice, exploitation, oppression, and violence (Freire 2017, 17–18). Societies, through these practices, according to Freire, make humans less human. He describes the humanity of the human animal as stolen by this process of dehumanisation, but absent even in those that have stolen the humanity of others.

In this way, the pedagogical practice that stands as the foundation of Freire's political theory, that which is the method by which people overthrow their oppression and realise their *conscientização*, begins with the beliefs and practices of the society in which the subject resides. It is in reference to the facts of one's own social environment, the beliefs and cultural practices of one's social environment that a person is introduced to the world and learns to re-interpret the world.

Rousseau, to a lesser extent, acknowledges this descriptive power also. In his search for universal value, he spends a great deal of time trying to work around it. It is not some ideal or pre-social animal that Rousseau considers in the move from the state of nature to one of cooperative association in *The Social Contract* but the human animal as it is – a corrupted and denatured creature. Furthermore, the invention of the Lawgiver and the isolation of Émile are aspects of his philosophy made necessary because of the corruption of the human animal by society, a force that Rousseau wants to overcome. The former, Rousseau places over and above the Sovereign until they are able to reliably access the General Will, and the latter with the aim of limiting Émile's access to other people and create an environment free form the corrupting and denaturing force of society. These examples are illustrative of Rousseau's understanding of the formative and coercive power of one's social environment.

The normative claims of the communitarian however are problematic. The communitarian is committed to the normative claim that the practices of a community to which people identify as members are in themselves valuable and should form the basis of our cultural, moral, and political values. It is here that I begin to distance myself from the communitarian argument. It may be the case that I place too much weight on the work that the word *should* is doing for the communitarian position but it is with the word *should* that I have the most concerns. Its use is either trivial or problematic. It seems strange to me because I think that it is the case that all people are members of a community and that community is constitutive of our moral and political beliefs – I think that it is unavoidable that this is the case. So, saying that it *should* be the case is like saying that we *should* identify as a human, or we *should* seek to identify with other people that we love and respect. This is not to say that I believe that all people are equally affected by their cultural and social surroundings, it is clear that many people do not feel drawn to the world in which they live, that they feel disconnected, adrift, yearning for something different to which they can relate and embrace, but even the most radical departure from the moral, political, and cultural beliefs of a person's social environment is still an example of a person that has been shaped by and understands the world through that social environment.

Therefore, because it seems absurd that the communitarian would be suggesting this trivial position, they must instead be asserting that attachment to one's community and the values and virtues of that community should be encouraged and sought. I think that this is the source of many people's concerns with communitarianism. This is why it is perceived as a socially conservative ideology because it is the underpinning of a model that is resistant to change and does not adequately value the challenges to the status quo from the next generation. Furthermore, it appears to support homogeneity and conflict without resolution: the former in the local community and the latter between those communities. These undesirable consequences are created by placing normative power on our attachment to our immediate social environment.

A further complication to communitarianism occurs when one considers that each person belongs not to one group but to many and that these groups will have overlapping but different moral, political, and cultural beliefs. How does the communitarian define the community? Is it simply the geographical area where we live and work or is it something more complex? Does a person who belongs to a Greek-Cypriot community and a local London Borough have to pick one of these groups to identify with, and if not how do they manage the conflicts that occur between them? What about a person who is active in the local school, rotary club, religious organisations, women's rights, or LGBTQ+ communities? Is this what the communitarian has in mind when they state that we should identify with our local community? This is obviously a complex web of associations and groups that have the potential to cause great internal conflict and does not seem like the strongest foundations for cooperative association – and only because of the *should*. It is making this a normative claim rather than merely a descriptive one that causes these problems.

Attached to this concern is the meta-ethical claim made by the communitarian. Caney attributes to communitarianism the meta-ethical claim "that correct moral principles mirror the shared understandings of communities" (Caney 1992, 286). Caney rejects this and for good reason. It commits us to some form of cultural relativism that puts communities into conflict with one another. Caney writes, "In some cases, following the shared values of one community will necessarily entail overriding the shared values of another community" (Caney 1992, 288). It is attributing 'correctness' to moral principles that is problematic and I want to encourage an attitude shift into the world of doubt. Doubt encourages reflection and moral growth, whereas the attachment to ideas of 'correct' or 'right' to our moral principles does quite the opposite. It teaches us to resist and defend, that is the source of conflict, dogma, and resistance to change.

In accepting the descriptive arguments of the communitarian and rejecting the normative, I argue that the necessary starting point of enquiry and one that sits in sharp contrast to the starting point of ideal theory which is often divorced from reality, is the point that moral values and virtues differ across communities, and while there is no consensus within any one community, there is a reasonably stable belief set that governs local policy and expectation. It is this social environment that shapes us and it is this that operates as the foundation for our moral discovery. In making it a descriptive claim – that we do identify, to a greater a lesser degree, with our local community; that we are framed by, and understand ourselves in reference to, our local community we create the surest foundation for political and social investigation.

Normatively cosmopolitan

The cosmopolitan theorist is committed to the view that each person is of equal moral worth and there is no justification for partial moral principles, which prioritise or elevate one group above another. Martha Nussbaum identifies the underlying moral principle of cosmopolitanism when she writes, "Whatever else we are bound by and pursue, we should recognise, at whatever personal or social cost, that each human being is human and counts as the moral equal of every other" (Nussbaum 2002b, 133). It is for this reason that the cosmopolitan citizen is often presented in opposition to the communitarian citizen, because the communitarian is often presented as possessing, and is most easily associated with, partiality towards one group above others, usually in reference to an individual's membership of a certain geographically defined community.

The roots of cosmopolitanism can be traced back to antiquity. Diogenes the Cynic expresses a cosmopolitan view, although he only professes it in the negative sense, i.e. one does not owe special duties to the state of which one resides. Stoics, such as Cicero and Seneca, also defend some form of moderate cosmopolitanism (Branham and Goulet-Cazé 2007; Hicks 2000, Vol. 2: 549–58). These roots have developed into at least three different branches of cosmopolitanism, but these branches, while interrelated, can come apart. There are political cosmopolitans, moral cosmopolitans, and economic cosmopolitans. Economic cosmopolitanism is the defence of free markets and attributable to people such as Adam Smith (1999a, 1999b). I understand a political cosmopolitan as a person who is committed to some form of world organising body. These bodies can be loosely federated or, in some cases, a world state is defended. Parts of Kant's political philosophy are illustrative of a model of political cosmopolitanism in this way (Kant 1991a, 1991b). This does not exclude the political sphere from moral and economic cosmopolitanism, it simply identifies a specific type of cosmopolitanism that is specifically engaging in the question of some form of world organising body. For the purposes of my argument, I want to focus on moral cosmopolitanism which can be understood as a commitment to universal moral principles which apply to all people equally. Influential ethical theorists like Kant and Bentham develop ethical systems of deontology and consequentialism, respectively, which are just this – ethical models that apply to all people equally (Bentham 2007; Kant 2012).

All forms of cosmopolitanism are subject to a set of criticisms that centre around the anchor of their principles. If one does not owe special allegiance to the state or the people of the state in which one resides, then to what does one owe that allegiance. It is argued that it is not possible to consider oneself a citizen of the world in the same way as a person considers themselves to be a citizen of a nation-state because there is too little to motivate the moral connection to the world. Walzer writes, "I am not a citizen of the world ... I am not even aware that there is a world such that one could be a citizen of it" (Walzer 2002, 125). This objection to cosmopolitanism argues that, in the case of the nation-state, the people of that nation-state share a history, culture, values, and respect for the rule of law of that nation-state, while this is not the case for the world. It is thought that there is too little to motivate the necessary empathy to ground a commitment of equal moral worth in the way demanded by the cosmopolitan. This is a problematic claim; it is not clear that the nation-state satisfies the conditions set either, but it seems that it has a greater chance of satisfying them than the cosmopolitan. Walzer objects to cosmopolitanism on these grounds. He writes, "I have commitments beyond the borders of this or any other country, to fellow Jews, say, or to social democrats around the world, or to people in trouble in faraway countries, but these are not citizen-like commitments" (Walzer 2002, 126).

Connected to Walzer's point is that, by-and-large, a person will feel greater empathy and attachment to those geographically proximal and to those who they can immediately relate to, such as their family and friends. It is highly likely that the vast majority of these people will be fellow citizens. Therefore, there is the practical fact that we share an organisational structure and there is the emotional fact that we share a bond with those closest to us.

These objections fail to adequately address the cosmopolitan claim because they do not address the moral claim. They are objections to the practicality of a cosmopolitan ethic not a refutation of the moral principles that underpin that ethic, and they only succeed in expressing a counter-intuition. It may be the case that people are not much motivated to place equal moral weight to all persons, and to care about distant others the way they care about those close to them. However, the cosmopolitan does not claim that people *do*, the cosmopolitan claims that we *should* care about the people of the world in this way and that we are mistaken in prioritising fellow citizens simply because they are our fellow citizens.

Nussbaum develops an account of cosmopolitanism that shows us how we can move towards a state of affairs that realises the cosmopolitan ideal. Influenced by the cosmopolitanism of Stoicism, Nussbaum provides an account of moral practice that reimagines the concentric circles of moral attachment. The idea is that each person identifies with spheres of association that represent their moral commitments. She writes,

> The first one encircles the self, the next takes in the immediate family, then, in order, neighbours or local groups, fellow city-dwellers, and fellow countrymen – and we can easily add to this list groupings based on ethnic, linguistic, historical, professional, gender, or sexual identities. Outside all these circles is the largest one, humanity as a whole.
>
> (Nussbaum 2002a, 9)

However, these circles are descriptive, and they need not be understood as objective or fixed. The circles provide an illustrative function in that they highlight a plausible ordering of moral partialism. A different order with different categories does not affect the cosmopolitan argument. This is because after recognising that people possess a weighted morality based upon concentric circles, the cosmopolitan goes on to argue that the normative aim is to draw these circles together. Nussbaum achieves this end through a defence of cosmopolitan education which is designed to put people into conversation with the world.

Dewey shared these cosmopolitan commitments. David T. Hansen notes, "the provenance of his thought had no national or otherwise predetermined boundaries, and … the meanings in his thought were not pre-shaped by wherever his desk and typewriter happened to be" (Hansen 2009, 126). Leonard J. Waks also notes a cosmopolitan strain in Dewey's thought. He writes, "While Dewey does not often use the terms cosmopolitan and cosmopolitanism, the notions play an essential role in his mature viewpoint" (Waks 2009, 117).

According to Hansen, Dewey's cosmopolitanism is present in the enquiry that takes place by individuals of and with the world. It is found in Dewey's understanding of the human animal as fluid and revisable. Hansen writes that,

> In his view, a person is not a finished, complete, or fixed entity, however much the person's habits may run in a steady rhythm or well-worn grove. Rather a person, in principle, is in fact in continuous formation through the crucible of what he or she participates in and the manner or style in which he or she participates.
>
> (Hansen 2009, 128)

This is a cosmopolitan position because it does not assume a Cartesian foundation of knowledge, but a commitment to learning from all the contacts of life (Hansen 2009, 129). Dewey's cosmopolitanism is informed by his pragmatic method which determines a foundation of enquiry and growth. I find this and Nussbaum's educative commitment to drawing the spheres of association together, wholly persuasive. Not only does it tap directly into my moral intuitions with respect to the scope and function of morality and provide a theoretical foundation on which to build the cosmopolitan ethic through education, but it stands as a surer and more coherent foundation for moral and political enquiry if a principle of equality has been asserted.

An active participant in society

A third component of the citizen that operates as the end-in-view of a political project that follows in the tradition that I have sought to establish through Rousseau, Dewey, and Freire is that they must be active participants in society. The idea is that it is through participation that citizens are able to shape society to meet the cultural, social, and political values that they hold. At its most basic, this is found in the act of voting in local and national elections, but the ideal of participation goes much further than this, and if cultivated well, it is hoped that the links between the citizenry and their democratic representatives can be drawn much tighter, or even dissolved into a model of direct democracy.

Participatory democratic theory argues that cultivating greater participation within society at a young age results in greater participation within society throughout one's life. This is because the members of society learn and develop the skills of active participation in society by actively participating in society. Michael E. Morrell writes, "According to participatory democratic theory, citizens should be given greater opportunities to participate in making the decisions that govern their lives; if this were to happen, citizens would be transformed in positive ways" (Morrell 1999, 294). This is just one claim of the participatory democratic theorist however. Carole Pateman argues that, in addition to the claim that individuals learn to participate by participating that, "participatory democratic theory is an argument about democratisation" (Pateman 2012, 10). That is, the participatory democratic theorist identifies a number of ways in which society will be democratic and engage the individuals of society in politically active ways. Pateman defends participation as a value that is guaranteed by right. She writes,

> ... the conception of citizenship embodied in participatory democratic theory is that citizens are not at all like consumers. Citizens have the right to public provision, the right to participate in decision-making about their collective life and to live within authority structures that make such participation possible.
>
> (Pateman 2012, 15)

Pateman, inspired by the works of Rousseau and Mill, argues alongside them that greater participation will lead to greater acceptance of the dictates of society. But further to this, Pateman argues that participatory democracy has a positive impact on the education of those who participate and their integration into society. Pateman claims that evidence suggests, "we do learn to participate by participating and that feelings of political efficacy are more likely to be developed in a participatory environment" (Pateman 2000, 105). Morrell also takes up the mantle of participatory democracy. He writes, "participation, in order to increase citizens' positive perceptions of the decision-making process, must occur fairly often, involve several issues, and be structured so that citizens feel safe to offer their political opinions" (Morrell 1999, 294).

It is important to remember, however, that participation as a value risks becoming empty if that participation is not accompanied by something more. Participation in an unjust society or institutional framework is arguably contrary to the aims of the participatory democratic theorist. Participatory democratic theory argues for the democratisation of society and structural changes in the construct of society in order to facilitate greater democracy. In Pateman's words, the participatory society "needs to be created" (Pateman 2012, 10).

A commitment to participatory democracy is not universally shared. According to Dennis F. Thompson, "the most common empirical challenge to participatory theory" is that it is unrealistic, "because most citizens are not political animals" (Thompson 2008, 512). On this view, the participatory citizen is simply too demanding as an aim because most people do not want to participate in politics. However, this misses the point of participatory democratic theory. There is no claim that people are naturally or intrinsically political animals only that active participation is valuable in itself and ought to be cultivated because of that value. Thompson notes that participatory democratic theory is designed to challenge political reality, not accept it as given (Thompson 2008, 499 & 512).

A better objection, according to Thompson, seeks to show conflict between core values. Participation alone cannot build the attachments necessary for a functioning society of responsible citizens; therefore, there must be other values, such as deliberation, which are central to this vision of the citizen, and if this is so, then it must be explored so that the set of values is coherent. Adrian Oldfield addresses this concern and writes, "Political participation enlarges the minds of individuals, familiarises them with interests which lie beyond the immediacy of personal circumstance and environment, and encourages them to acknowledge that public concerns are the proper ones to which they should pay attention" (Oldfield 1990, 184). However, this is only a starting point because without some appeal to individual interests, it is likely that a significant portion of the populace would be resistant to developing the desired habits (Oldfield 1990, 184). Participation may well be a necessary component of citizenship, but it does not appear to be sufficient for citizenship (Kymlicka and Norman 1994, 361).

In the participatory democratic citizen, Rousseau is a primary classical source (Cook and Morgan 1971; Pateman 2000). Rousseau's political vision places the citizen at the centre of the political process. Every member of the citizenry is a part of the Sovereign body of Rousseau's Republic. The role of this Sovereign body is to act as the legislative power through the expression of the General Will. Rousseau writes, "Only those who are forming an association have the right to regulate the conditions of the society" (*OC III*, 380; *CWR Vol. 4*, 154). Rousseau argues that the citizens of the Republic will learn, through their participation as Sovereign, to express the General Will effectively and without error. But this will not happen straight away, nor will it happen unless the citizens participate in society as Sovereign (*OC III*, 438; *CWR Vol. 4*, 198–199).

Dewey's theory of democracy is also a model of participatory democracy. Joel Westheimer and Joseph Kahne write that Dewey, "emphasized participation in collective endeavours. To support the efficacy of these collective efforts, he also emphasized commitments to communication, experimentation, and scientifically informed dialogues" (Westheimer and Kahne 2004, 241). A main feature of Dewey's political project is an attempt to refine and maximise democracy within society as a tool for social change and enfranchisement of the individual. Dewey understood democracy not merely as the act of voting but as a process to be participated in by all, and as such, his political project immediately expands beyond that of political science and demands engagement with broad and complex philosophical and pedagogical problems. What Dewey provides instead of a fixed model of the ideal state is the method by which the structure and terms of association of the state meet the needs and desires of the citizenry. The method is Dewey's instrumentalism. He writes,

> To learn to be human is to develop through the give-and-take of communication an effective sense of being an individually distinctive member of a community; one who understands and appreciates its beliefs, desires and methods, and who contributes to a further conversion of organic powers into human resources and values. But this translation is never finished.
>
> (Dewey 1984, 332)

Communication in this way serves to support societal growth. This has an educative effect for the individual too. Sandra B. Rosenthal writes, "The educative effect of democratic participation, in Dewey's view, goes beyond skills and knowledge to involve moral development, and thus, personal transformation" (1986, 191). Dewey's theory of schooling and education links together what goes on in our homes and schools with society. For Dewey, a democratic person must possess the skills and desire to participate in society, and it was the responsibility of society to cultivate those qualities. This view can be seen in Dewey's writings very early, and it persists throughout his career. Dewey argued that the school, as a part of the community, must be involved in the community. Furthermore, it was Dewey's contention that the students of the school develop the skills and knowledge necessary by direct practice and observation. Therefore, greater interaction between school and society is encouraged. Within Deweyan scholarship, Dewey is widely thought of as a participatory democratic theorist (Westbrook 2010).

Possessor of rights and responsibilities

The last component of the citizen that I identify is that they be a possessor of both rights and responsibilities. This is almost trivially true in that without rights and responsibilities, there is little to secure the foundation of the three previous components. However, it bears well to state it clearly because it is here that we can see the origins of both the concept of the citizen and the earliest acknowledged tension within it.

The classical debate places the republican citizen and the liberal citizen in opposition with one another. A clear expression of the republican model can be found in the pages of *Émile*. Rousseau writes, "The Lacadaemonian Pedaretus runs for the council of three hundred. He is defeated. He goes home delighted that there were three hundred men worthier than he to be found in Sparta .... Behold the citizen" (*OC IV*, 249; *CWR Vol. 13*, 164). The person that places the interests of the state above their own is a citizen. This example seems almost naïve because something distinctly human is lost in Pedaretus' reaction and even more so when we think of the other example that Rousseau gives of a mother who loses her sons to war and cares more for victory (*OC IV*, 249; *CWR Vol. 13*, 164).

The republican conception of citizenship has seen a return in popularity in the second half of the twentieth century. In *The Human Condition*, Hannah Arendt challenges us to learn from the civilisations of the past. Ancient Greece provides the backdrop for challenging political assumptions taken for granted in the twentieth century (Arendt 1998). Quentin Skinner and Philip Pettit have also been hugely influential in reinvigorating the civic republican tradition. Skinner (1992) turns to Renaissance political thought, in particular drawing upon Machiavelli's *Discourses on Livy*. From this starting place, Skinner argues that the maximisation of liberty and the common good are compatible. He writes, "if we wish to maximize our liberty, we must devote ourselves wholeheartedly to a life of public service, placing the ideal of the common good above all considerations of individual advantage" (Skinner 1992, 217). The thought is that a free state, if guided by "the general will of the whole body politic," is therefore an expression of the freedom of each individual member of that body politic (Skinner 1992, 217).

   In a different, but still strongly republican vein, Pettit argues that freedom should be understood in terms of non-domination rather than non-interference. He writes, "someone dominates or subjugates another, to the extent that (1) they have the capacity to interfere (2) with impunity and at will (3) in certain choices that the other is in a position to make" (Pettit 1996, 578). Therefore, the state must not arbitrarily interfere in the lives of individuals because it would unjustly limit their freedom. What constitutes arbitrary interference is a matter of debate, but the paradigm example of the dominated individual is a slave. It is true that with a benevolent master, a slave could achieve seeming freedom and fulfil the conditions of freedom in the negative sense; however, the slave's master retains a power of arbitrary interference that may be employed at any time. Therefore, a slave – no matter who their master is – can never be free (Pettit 1996, 577). Skinner and Pettit argue that an appropriately democratic state can possess non-arbitrary power which is by definition not a constraint upon a person's freedom and in this way argue that the republican citizen and individual freedom are compatible. However, the republican conception of the citizen which emphasises the responsibilities of the citizenry is contrasted with a different model that emphasises the rights of each member of that citizen body: the liberal citizen.
   The liberal tradition shifts the focus of the citizen away from the responsibilities that they hold towards the state, and towards the rights possessed by the individual that are protected by the state. T. H. Marshall's influential essay 'Citizenship and Social Class' is illustrative of this conception of the citizen (Marshall 1950). Derek Heater refers to this essay as, "the most famous single work to have been composed on liberal citizenship" (Heater 1999, 12). Kymlicka and Norman similarly recognise the importance of this work. They write, "The most influential exposition of this postwar conception of citizen-as-rights is T. H. Marshall's 'Citizenship and Social Class'" (Kymlicka and Norman 1994, 354). According to Marshall, it is the advance of social policy – such as access to education, health, and minimum standard of living – that leads to an equalising of status among the populace. Marshall writes,

> ... in the twentieth century citizenship and the capitalist class system have been at war. ... Social rights in their modern form imply an invasion of contract by status, the subordination of market price to social justice, the replacement of the free bargain by the declaration of rights.
> (Marshall 1950, 68)

This is characteristic of liberal citizenship because it is argued that in equalising status among people it is more probable that they will feel like full members of society and act as such. It is clear from this that Marshall emphasises the role of rights in his conception of citizenship and argues that in securing rights people will take ownership of their citizenship. The liberal conception of the citizen changes the focus away from the public sphere and the virtues that promote the public good, to the private sphere and the rights of the individual to live without interference by the state within that sphere. Walzer writes of the liberal citizen, "For them, the political community is only a necessary framework, a set of external arrangements, not a common life" (Walzer 1989, 215–16).

The conceptions of the republican citizen of active responsibilities in the public sphere and the liberal citizen of passive rights in the private sphere are not dichotomous. This is something acknowledged by the defenders of both the republican and the liberal citizen. The republican citizen, while primarily focussed on the responsibilities felt, must also recognise the importance of rights within this conception, whether this be in the minimal sense of a central commitment to a right of non-domination or something more, in order to secure the active participation of the citizenry. Similarly, within the liberal conception of the citizen, Marshall writes,

> If citizenship is invoked in the defence of rights, the corresponding duties of citizenship cannot be ignored. These do not require a man to sacrifice his individual liberty or to submit without question to every demand made by government. But they do require that his acts should be inspired by a lively sense of responsibility towards the welfare of the community.
>
> (Marshall 1950, 70)

In light of this, some have suggested that the republican and liberal conceptions of the citizen are complementary (Ackerman 2003; Walzer 1989). We can see how the liberal and republican conceptions of the citizen begin to cohere when we understand them through their respective commitments to responsibilities or rights in the objections that are raised against them. What we are left with in the debate between the republican and liberal conceptions of the citizen is the reiteration of the tension between the individual and society that started the book. Therefore, I make the trivial commitment to the citizen that operates as the end-in-view as being a bearer of both rights and responsibilities and employ the other components that I have identified of this citizen for the purposes of providing a moral foundation on which these rights and responsibilities rest as well as the environment necessary to discover what form these rights and responsibilities will take.

Marshall thought that the assumption of responsibilities through active participation would occur as a direct result of a person's citizenship rights, but it is not clear that this is the case. If active participation does not occur as a result of granting the conditions in which a person can assume responsibilities, and it is necessary for the stable functioning of a cooperative society that a citizen has both rights and responsibilities, then it must be established how these responsibilities are cultivated. This is what I intend to do, we will hopefully see over the course of the subsequent chapters a defence of the necessary conditions for the development of a person who will voluntarily assume the responsibilities of the citizen without ceding their individual freedom.

Conclusion

The political agent that operates as the end-in-view of a project that follows in the tradition that I have sought to establish through Rousseau, Dewey, and Freire is best understood as descriptively communitarian, normatively cosmopolitan, an active participant in one's society, and a possessor of rights and responsibilities. I call this political agent the Critical Citizen.

Each component, taken together, is asserted as a consequence of the methodology that I established in Chapter 1. This is sometimes explicit as is the case with the communitarian and participatory aspects of the citizen; and it is sometimes implicit, as is the case with the commitment to the cosmopolitan ethic which I believe is a consequence of thorough application of the method. I believe that this can be seen more clearly when the key aspects of the methodology that I employ are made explicit. In the most basic sense, from Rousseau, we learn the importance of a dual project, one which engages at the interactional and institutional level, where society is developed for the citizen as the citizen develops for society; from Dewey, we learn the importance of the interconnectedness of means and ends as the foundation of method; and from Freire, we learn the value in problematising and challenging existing ways of life through problem-posing education. The Critical Citizen, therefore, is not something that ends at a certain point in one's life but a project that continues over the course of many generations as we learn and develop together. It is a concept of lifelong learning and an inter-generational project that continues to develop with the fluctuations of time and morality. Furthermore, it is realised through two avenues, the institutional and interactional; they must develop and exist within an environment which is sensitive to the interconnectedness of means and ends; and they must be subject to the lifelong pursuit of education through a problem-posing model.

The concept of the Critical Citizen is one that holds the value of equal moral worth; is the product of an education which is dialogical; and a member of a society which is constructed in accordance with these two principles and therefore educative in itself. So conceived, the Critical Citizen is an ongoing process without fixed end but the end-in-view of educative growth and humanisation. One can be a citizen in their own time and place, but as a result of the educative process, they are a citizen only at that time and place. They will not meet the criteria of 'citizen' in this strict sense as the conditions of one's social environment change unless they too change. We, however, in the present context of Western values and hegemony, I feel reasonably confident in asserting, do not fulfil the criteria laid out above. We are, at best, partial citizens, oppressed, and oppressors alike. The rest of this book, having now established method, aim, and judgement, will apply the method defended and develop a positive thesis that will elucidate what is necessary to realise our end-in-view.

References

Ackerman, Bruce. 2003. 'Neo-Federalism?' In *Constitutionalism and Democracy*, edited by Jon Elster and Rune Slagstad, 153–94. Studies in Rationality and Social Change. Cambridge: Cambridge University Press.

Arendt, Hannah. 1998. *The Human Condition*. 2nd ed. Chicago, IL: University of Chicago Press.

Bentham, Jeremy. 2007. *An Introduction to the Principles of Morals and Legislation*. Mineola, NY: Dover Publications.

Branham, Robert Bracht, and Marie-Odile Goulet-Cazé, eds. 2007. *The Cynics: The Cynic Movement in Antiquity and Its Legacy: 23*. Berkeley: University of California Press.

Caney, Simon. 1992. 'Liberalism and Communitarianism: A Misconceived Debate'. *Political Studies* 40 (2): 273–89. https://doi.org/10.1111/j.1467-9248.1992.tb01384.x

Cook, Terrence E., and Patrick M. Morgan. 1971. *Participatory Democracy*. San Francisco, CA: Canfield Press.

Dewey, John. 1984. 'The Public and Its Problems'. In *The Later Works of John Dewey, 1925–1953, Volume 2: 1925–1927*, edited by Jo Ann Boydston, 235–372. Carbondale: Southern Illinois University Press.

Diogenes Laertius. 2018. *Lives of the Eminent Philosophers*. Translated by Pamela Mensch. New York: Oxford University Press.

Freire, Paulo. 2017. *Pedagogy of the Oppressed*. Translated by Myra Bergman Ramos. London: Penguin Books.

Hansen, David T. 2009. 'Dewey and Cosmopolitanism'. *Education and Culture* 25 (2): 126–40.

Heater, Derek Benjamin. 1999. *What Is Citizenship?* Malden, MA: Polity Press.

Hicks, Robert Drew. 2000. *Lives of Eminent Philosophers*. Vol. 2. The Loeb Classical Library. London: Heinemann.

Kant, Immanuel. 1991a. 'Idea for a Universal History with a Cosmopolitan Purpose'. In *Kant: Political Writings*, edited by Hans Siegbert Reiss, 2nd ed., 41–53. Cambridge Texts in the History of Political Thought. Cambridge; New York: Cambridge University Press.

Kant, Immanuel. 1991b. 'Perpetual Peace: A Philosophical Sketch'. In *Kant: Political Writings*, edited by Hans Siegbert Reiss, 2nd ed., 93–130. Cambridge Texts in the History of Political Thought. Cambridge; New York: Cambridge University Press.

Kant, Immanuel. 2012. *Groundwork of the Metaphysics of Morals*. Edited by Mary J. Gregor and Jens Timmermann. Rev ed. Cambridge Texts in the History of Political Thought. Cambridge: Cambridge University Press.

Kymlicka, Will, and Wayne Norman. 1994. 'Return of the Citizen: A Survey of Recent Work on Citizenship Theory'. *Ethics* 104 (2): 352–81. https://doi.org/10.1086/293605

MacIntyre, Alasdair C. 1978. *Against the Self-Images of the Age: Essays on Ideology and Philosophy*. Notre Dame, IN: University of Notre Dame Press.

Marshall, T. H. 1950. 'Citizenship and Social Class'. In *Citizenship and Social Class and Other Essays*, 1–85. London; New York: Cambridge University Press.

McCowan, Tristan. 2009. *Rethinking Citizenship Education: A Curriculum for Participatory Democracy*. Continuum Studies in Educational Research. London; New York: Continuum.

Morrell, Michael E. 1999. 'Citizen's Evaluations of Participatory Democratic Procedures: Normative Theory Meets Empirical Science'. *Political Research Quarterly* 52 (2): 293–322.

Nussbaum, Martha Craven. 2002a. 'Patriotism and Cosmopolitanism'. In *For Love of Country? Debating the Limits of Patriotism*, edited by Joshua Cohen, 2–20. Boston, MA: Beacon Press.

Nussbaum, Martha Craven. 2002b. 'Reply'. In *For Love of Country? Debating the Limits of Patriotism*, edited by Joshua Cohen, 131–44. Boston, MA: Beacon Press.

Oldfield, Adrian. 1990. 'Citizenship: An Unnatural Practice?' *The Political Quarterly* 61 (2): 177–87.

Pateman, Carole. 2000. *Participation and Democratic Theory*. Reprinted. Cambridge: Cambridge University Press.

Pateman, Carole. 2012. 'Participatory Democracy Revisited'. *Perspectives on Politics* 10 (01): 7–19.

Pettit, Philip. 1996. 'Freedom as Antipower'. *Ethics* 106 (3): 576–604.

Rawls, John. 1999. *A Theory of Justice*. Rev. ed. Cambridge, MA: Belknap Press of Harvard University Press.

Rosenthal, Sandra B. 1986. *Speculative Pragmatism*. Amherst: University of Massachusetts Press.

Rousseau, Jean-Jacques. 1994. *Social Contract; Discourse on the Virtue Most Necessary for a Hero; Political Fragments; and, Geneva Manuscript*. Edited by Roger D. Masters, Christopher Kelly, and Judith R. Bush. The Collected Writings of Rousseau, Vol. 4. Hanover: University Press of New England.

Rousseau, Jean-Jacques. 1999. *Émile. Éducation. Morale. Botanique*. Œuvres Complètes, IV. Paris: Gallimard.

Rousseau, Jean-Jacques. 2003. *Du contrat social. Écrits politiques*. Edited by Bernard Gagnebin and François Bouchardy. Œuvres Complètes, III. Paris: Gallimard.

Rousseau, Jean-Jacques. 2010. *Emile, or, On Education: Includes Émile and Sophie, or, The Solitaries*. Edited by Christopher Kelly. Translated by Allan Bloom. The Collected Writings of Rousseau, Vol. 13. Hanover: University Press of New England.

Skinner, Quentin. 1992. 'On Justice, the Common Good, and Priority of Liberty'. In *Dimensions of Radical Democracy: Pluralism, Citizenship, Community*, edited by Chantal Mouffe, 211–24. Phronesis Series. London; New York: Verso.

Smith, Adam. 1999a. *The Wealth of Nations: Books I–III*. Reprinted. Penguin Classics. London; New York: Penguin Books.

Smith, Adam. 1999b. *The Wealth of Nations: Books IV–V*. Penguin Classics. London; New York: Penguin Books.

Taylor, Charles. 1985. 'Interpretation and the Sciences of Man'. In *Philosophy and the Human Sciences: Philosophical Papers 2*, 15–57. Cambridge; New York: Cambridge University Press.

Taylor, Charles.1989. *Sources of the Self: The Making of the Modern Identity*. Cambridge, MA: Harvard University Press.

The Marriage (Same Sex Couples) Act. 2013.

The Sexual Offences Act. 1967.

Select Committee on Citizenship and Civic Engagement, 'The Ties That Bind: Citizenship and Civic Engagement in the 21st Century' or The Ties That Bind. 2018.

Thompson, Dennis F. 2008. 'Deliberative Democratic Theory and Empirical Political Science'. *Annual Review of Political Science* 11 (1): 497–520.

Waks, Leonard J. 2009. 'Inquiry, Agency, and Art: John Dewey's Contribution to Pragmatic Cosmopolitanism'. *Education and Culture* 25 (2): 115–25.

Walzer, Michael. 1989. 'Citizenship'. In *Political Innovation and Conceptual Change*, edited by Terence Ball, James Farr, and Russell L. Hanson, 211–19. Ideas in Context. Cambridge; New York: Cambridge University Press.

Walzer, Michael. 2002. 'Spheres of Affection'. In *For Love of Country? Debating the Limits of Patriotism*, edited by Joshua Cohen, 125–27. Boston, MA: Beacon Press.

Westbrook, Robert Brett. 2010. *John Dewey and American Democracy*. Ithaca, NY: Cornell University Press.

Westheimer, Joel, and Joseph Kahne. 2004. 'What Kind of Citizen? The Politics of Educating for Democracy'. *American Educational Research Journal* 41 (2): 237–69.

Chapter 3

The individual, society, and the problem of authority

Introduction

In the previous chapter, I identified and defended a model of the individual that operates as the aim of education. In this chapter, I address the obstacles to its realisation. The Critical Citizen is defined by its positive relationship between the interests of the individual and the interests of society, and so, it is necessary to explore the tension that exists between these two groups, what is the root of that tension, and whether that tension can be resolved.

If you permit me to return briefly to the protagonists of my study, the respective politico-educational projects of Rousseau, Dewey, and Freire are very well placed to situate the next stage of the argument that I wish to develop, just as they were in the methodological foundation. The beauty of employing the projects established by Rousseau, Dewey, and Freire in the background of my treatise is that each, to some degree, employed a method of democratic education as a solution to the tension between the individual and society, saw the problem of authority as a key cause of the corruption of that tension; yet, each failed provide an adequate response to the problem of authority. Therefore, in this chapter, I shall use Rousseau, Dewey, and Freire as guideposts from the aim of education established in the previous chapter to a discussion of the obstacles faced in reaching that aim.

I shall show how Rousseau, Dewey, and Freire each developed a model of democratic education as an answer to the tension between the individual and society. Then, I shall show how the problem of authority remains in spite of their best efforts. This will lead into the next chapter where I introduce the interactional structure of education as the first path for the realisation of the Critical Citizen. But first, I shall elucidate what the problem of authority is and why it is a problem that may stand underneath the tension between the individual and society, prohibiting a suitable resolution.

Problem of authority

In the much hypothesised state of nature, prior to the advent of political organisation, the individual was the unit and the whole of moral and political

DOI: 10.4324/9781003271871-4

action. Whether understood as a heuristic device, a literal stage of the political development of the human animal, or something else, the state of nature offers a useful tool for comparison with cooperative association.

The trouble with state of nature theory is in the projected psychology of the human animal, and in consequence, the method and means by which we move from the state of nature into cooperative association. The classic comparison here is the differing psychologies hypothesised by John Locke (1980) and Thomas Hobbes (1988). Are we by nature, mostly cooperative and empathetic or are we selfish and primarily interested in our own preservation? Although I do possess strong views on this debate, I can happily sidestep its complications here because I only wish to suggest that outside of political union, the individual possesses both freedom and authority of themselves and their actions. It is in our capacity as members of a community or political state that these concepts become complicated. As noted in Chapter 1, the complication that requires an answer, in Rousseau's words, is to,

> ... find a form of association that defends and protects the person and goods of each associate with all the common force, and by means of which each one, uniting with all, nevertheless obeys only himself and remains as free as before.
>
> (OC III, 360; CWR, Vol. 4, 138)

Therefore, the problem of authority, as a key component of the tension between the individual and society, is to submit to the authority of cooperative association with others and yet retain individual freedom in spite of this submission. The problem of authority understood in this way is relatively simple. If authority is a necessary part of cooperative association, and the maximisation of freedom is an aim of cooperative association, then we must show how authority and freedom are compatible with one another. If authority and freedom are not compatible with one another, then we must do at least one of three things; sacrifice, to some degree, our individual freedom; reject the premise that authority is necessary within cooperative association; or abandon the aim of cooperative association. For the most part, people seek to show how freedom and authority are compatible. However, there are some who defend a more authoritarian balance of power in order to protect a limited or narrow conception of freedom. Immediately, the Leviathan state of Hobbes springs to mind. Conversely, there is the position of the anarchist or libertarian and their radical rejection of authority in the name of freedom. To these ideas, I shall return later in the chapter.

Rousseau, Dewey, and Freire like most political commentators were acutely aware of the tension between the individual and society, especially with regard to the relationship between authority and freedom within that tension. Rousseau, Dewey, and Freire each seek to address the troubling nature of authority in their political projects that seek to realise the freedom of the human animal. We can see how this manifested in the aim of Rousseau's political project above, but it is equally true of Dewey and Freire and each of them sought to address this tension through democratic education.

The resolution through democratic education

Rousseau, Dewey, and Freire each illustrate the value education as a part of political theory by placing learning, in particular of the skills and virtues needed for effective and successful participation in democratic society, at the heart of their political systems. The education received provides the foundations of democratic society for Rousseau, Dewey, and Freire. This is because for each of them democracy was more than the mere act of voting, and more than the mechanisms of government are needed to insulate the people of society from corruption, from being led astray, from bad or selfish decisions.

Rousseau envisaged small republic states that were ruled through direct democracy of its citizens, free from faction and self-interest. Instead, the citizens of Rousseau's republics are each members of the Sovereign and are guided by the General Will. By this, it is meant that each person independently and through reason considers and concludes the rules and policies of the Republic with their reason focussed on what is best for the Republic. Rousseau argues that in so doing the Sovereign will reach a mandate with a legitimate authority because those that disagree have failed to identify the General Will. Therefore, it is democratic governance with a focus on participation.

The educative elements of this system are twofold. Through the education of the individual found in *Émile*, a person is educated to be at first a free individual, and then, once they possess the virtues and strength needed to withstand the corruption of society, they are educated to be a citizen. Émile is educated to enter the social world and participate in it with the strength to withstand its corrupting and denaturing force, to not fall into factionalism, to not be led astray, to see with clarity, and to possess the fortitude to follow the mandates of reason.

Then, in *The Social Contract*, the citizen is educated through participation. They learn to do this over time and through practice. They are helped in this aim by the Lawgiver who acts as a parallel authority to the tutor. Where in *Émile* the tutor guides and instructs the young person as they develop, the Lawgiver guides and instructs the body of citizens as they develop. The Lawgiver is not a member of the Sovereign but is in a position to help the citizen body access and express the General Will, while they cannot do so unerringly themselves. A key method by which the Lawgiver achieves this aim is through the authority of God as a tool to lend authority to their own pronouncements. The Lawgiver uses the authority of God to compel the people of society to obey, "without violence and persuade without convincing"

(*OC III*, 383; *CWR*, *Vol. 4*, 156). God is then employed as a tool of control so that the guidance of the Lawgiver is accepted and followed. That control is hidden from the eyes and minds of the Sovereign. It is in this way, accompanied by the formative education of *Émile*, that the citizen is able to be guided by the General Will as a member of the Sovereign.

Rousseau addresses the tension between the interests of the individual and society through a division of the public and private spheres of a person's life and the incorporation of the individual into the authority of society. This is how Rousseau is able to answer his question: the human animal remains as free in cooperative association as they were in the state of nature by retaining that freedom in the private sphere. In matters that do not affect the interests of the state or the lives of other citizens, a person may do as they wish. Correspondingly, the cooperative association protects all members with common force by empowering them with the voice of the General Will.

Dewey's democratic education is deeply embedded in his political philosophy. Its roots are found in the schooling that we are to receive and it is continued throughout our lives as we engage meaningfully in our community through thought and action. It is best represented by his practical endeavour into education and schooling. During his tenure at the University of Chicago, a primary school, commonly known as the Lab School or the Dewey School, was established under his guidance. The purpose of this school was twofold, to contribute educational theory through analysis of practice and to contribute to the knowledge of educational practice through experiment (Dewey 1976b). The main principle of the Lab School was to create a, "miniature community, an embryonic society" (Dewey 1976a, 12). Therefore, Dewey's Lab School is an expression of democratic education because it aimed to develop a participatory democratic school. Liba H. Engel writes, "The purpose was not to provide children with unbridled freedom but to help them grow toward effective social membership" (2008, 118).

The principles of the school were worked out by the teachers cooperatively and through trial and error. Within the limits of the general principle of the school as an embryonic community with an emphasis on the connection between learning and active work, "the development of concrete material and of methods for dealing with it was wholly in the hands of the teachers" (Mayhew and Edwards 2007, 367). There were weekly teachers' meetings in which the prior week's experiences were discussed in the context of the general plan. The plan would be modified and adapted in light of the difficulties faced. The meetings "translated" the abstract theory into the concrete teaching experiences and created a feedback loop between the two in an example of cooperative teaching practice and a practical example of Deweyan pragmatic communal enquiry.

In Dewey's Lab School, the education provided was directed by the students' interests through the professional expertise of the teachers. At the Lab School, they did not teach discrete subjects. The concern was that by separating subjects out into separate bodies of knowledge, the content becomes abstract and divorced from the world of the student, thereby making the information difficult to process and contrary to the desires of the student (Dewey 2008b). The alternative that Dewey proposes is what he refers to as occupations. They are a different way of understanding how to organise and classify the knowledge and skills developed in a school. Instead of a body of knowledge classified by type and packaged as a discrete subject like Mathematics, English, History, etc., Dewey repackages the information as a part of the interests of the student. Through occupations, learning becomes concrete and relatable. Liba H. Engel writes, "a geographical or historical fact must be something the child can incorporate into his or her actions" (2008, 119). Therefore, following the interest of the child, it was by occupations that Dewey organised a student's education. Through occupations, a student will be introduced to all subjects.

Dewey's pedagogical practice is clearly a reflection of this as the teachers continually reflect on the student's needs and desires and frame their practice around these relatively stable but fluid ends. Similarly, this process takes place at the larger societal level also because the aim is that the form and values of society will shift over time through the continual re-evaluation of ends (Dewey 1984, 245–61). His educational practice was therefore democratic because it aimed to break down the boundaries between school and community, encouraging the students to be members of that community, and engaging in the communal inquiry which sought change for better and for all. The students of the Lab School were becoming, through practice, participants in a democratic society (Dewey 2008a, 93).

This practice extended beyond formal education and explicitly into the political sphere. All members of society are encouraged to participate in the discussions that guide policy in society at large, guided by the expertise of public officials who operate in the interests of all members of society. What Dewey provides is the method by which the structure and terms of association of the state meet the needs and desires of the citizenry. Dewey writes,

… popular government is educative as other modes of political regulation are not. It forces a recognition that there are common interests, even though recognition of what they are is confused; and the need it enforces of discussion and publicity brings about some clarification of what they are.

(Dewey 1984, 364)

This is because democratic governance is, according to Dewey, the most capable model of governance of supporting pragmatic enquiry. It provides the institutional structure needed for the development of persons and the societies of which they are a part. It is able to support this societal growth only if the members of that society actively participate within it, and these participatory skills are learned through the practice of those skills.

Dewey's vision of democracy focuses on the breaking down of the barriers between the school and society, between the school and the family, and between the individual and the external forces which arrest humanisation or educative growth. This is true of Freire as well however, unlike Dewey, the Freirean model of democratic education attempts to resist the path towards the authority of expertise as a legitimate source.

For Freire, the destructive form of authority practised by the oppressors remains a historical fact. Both the oppressors and the oppressed recognise this authority and act in accordance with it. However, this is not a legitimate manifestation of authority according to Freire because its foundations are built upon the fear of freedom. In fact, Freire goes as far as arguing that the existing social order perpetuates the oppressor–oppressed dynamic and therefore must be challenged through a radical and revolutionary pedagogy which reinterprets the world. As can be seen in the process described above, this is not something that can be easily undone and the student–teacher must continue to question and challenge the world around them and their understanding of it. As Freire states, "Knowledge emerges only through invention and re-invention, through the restless, impatient, continuing, hopeful inquiry human beings pursue in the world, with the world, and with each other" (2017, 45).

I have introduced Freire's problem-posing education in Chapter 1. Accompanying this pedagogical theory are Freire's revolutionary educators and his educational practice. The tool to help the oppressed overcome their oppression and realise their freedom is the educator. The educator is participating in the revolution by providing the space and the opportunity for the oppressed to revolt; therefore, they are the revolutionary leaders. To be a revolutionary leader, one must fulfil two criteria. First, one must be genuinely committed to the revolutionary cause; and second, one must participate in the subversion of the role of the teacher by not assuming authority in virtue of their status as a teacher but to earn that authority through communication (Freire 2017, 83, 84). With respect to the former, this means that the revolutionary educator must trust the oppressed to discover their oppression and seek to overcome it. Freire writes,

> The correct method for a revolutionary leadership to employ in the task of liberation ... lies in dialogue. The conviction of the oppressed that they must fight for their liberation is not a gift bestowed by the revolutionary leadership, but the result of their own conscientização.
>
> (2017, 41)

The Freirean teacher–student, if coming from the oppressor class, must submit to a "profound rebirth"; they must be one with the oppressed and they cannot be so as long as they hold on to the identity of their privilege.

Elsewhere, Freire describes this movement variously as an "Easter experience" (1984, 525) and as "class suicide" (1978, 10). These terms are all referring to the same thing; the overcoming of one's particular world view in favour of the world view of the oppressed. In Freire's words, "Those who undergo it must take on a new form of existence; they can no longer remain as they were" (2017, 35). If this is not done, there remains a distinct risk that a person who was once oppressor may bring with them attitudes and assumptions exclusive to that class. Furthermore, they may, despite their genuine desire to bring about social justice, seek to do so on behalf of the oppressed rather than together with them. Freire writes that, "A real humanist can be identified more by his trust in the people, which engages him in their struggle, than by a thousand actions in their favour without that trust" (2017, 34).

The revolutionary leader aims to cultivate new knowledge and new understandings of the world by encouraging an attitude of reflection and dialogue amongst members of a community. They are sensitive to the particular circumstances and context of the students and illicit the learning stimuli from the community of the students, "with an attitude of understanding towards what they see" (Freire 2017, 83). In doing so, the revolutionary leaders impose stimuli upon the students but cultivate that stimuli from the students. They are, therefore, sympathetic to the nuances and particularities of each community, and the stimuli are presented to the students, not as answers to be remembered and adhered to "but as problems to be solved" (Freire 2017, 96). In this way, pre-existing knowledge is problematised and critiqued without an imposition from some epistemic authority.

Freire's educational work extended beyond the interactional, and he was heavily involved in the institutional design and structure of education as well. When he returned from exile to Brazil, Freire soon became the Municipal Secretary of Education in São Paulo and was responsible for 662 schools with 720,000 students from early years to 13–14 years of age, as well as leading adult education and literacy training. In 1989, he proposed a democratic education programme which aimed to develop responsible and critical citizens and widen access and participation in school (Schugurensky 2012). This was exemplified in Freire's escola cidadã or Citizen School. Schugurensky writes, "Through this project, Freire continued his proposals for popular education, but in the context of the public school and in relation to reforms in the school administration, pedagogical planning, curricular organisation, and school evaluation" (2012, 52).

The Citizen School aimed to provide a model of dialogical education at both interactional and institutional levels through, "more dialogical relations in the classroom and more democratic forms of management, including partnerships with local groups and with parents, with a view to participatory decision processes in terms of planning, implementation, and allocation of resources" (Schugurensky 2012, 52). It was thought that this would increase the level of autonomy of schools and the level of responsibility of the local community for their schools, thereby ensuring a greater transparency of policies which were influenced by both school and government. This was achieved through policies such as the election of the principle and vice principle of the school where parents and children received fifty percent of the electoral weight and the teachers and staff the other fifty percent. Any elected administrator was then limited to a maximum of two terms in office.

Through the interactional pedagogical practice of the revolutionary educators and the institutional model of education evidenced by the escola cidadã, Freire developed a model of education which was participatory, political, and a force of social change through reflection and dialogue. This is Freire's model of democratic education.

The problem of authority – as it is and as it remains

Rousseau, Dewey, and Freire took great pains to address the problem of authority within their respective politico-educational projects. A large part of their answers to this problem and in turn the tension between the individual and society was to be led by their models of democratic education. Something that they all share and that permeates throughout each of their respective politico-educational theories is the commitment to participation accompanying education as the tool to political and individual freedom and the dissolution of the problematic tension between the individual and society. This fact was noted in the previous chapter and laid the foundation for democratic participation being considered a necessary condition of the Critical Citizen.

Yet, each of them struggled to create a practical solution that could move the human animal from its place in society as it is – corrupted, denatured, dehumanised, and oppressed – to the human animal in the reimagined world without compromising on the values that are meant to guide that reimagined world. Although the problem of authority is something that they each recognised and sought to answer, it is a problem that not one of them fully escaped. The challenges presented by the problem of authority in their work are indicative of how the problem of authority continues to stall attempts to address the tension between the individual and society that persists within all forms of cooperative association. Therefore, Rousseau, Dewey, and Freire continue to provide useful guideposts as we establish the scope and intricacies of the problem that I wish to answer.

Rousseauian authority is found both in external sources and in oneself. Externally, authority is found in the tutor, in the Lawgiver, and in God. In oneself, authority is found both when a member of the state of nature and as Sovereign in the Republic. The problem with Rousseau's formulation of external authority is with the realisation of a being capable of assuming the role. For Émile's tutor to have legitimate authority in the role of educator, they must be invented and assumed. No living person can fulfil the necessary and sufficient criteria of the tutor. This is also the case with the Lawgiver of *The Social Contract*. The function and necessity of the Lawgiver mirror the function and necessity of the tutor, and both are fictions. Therefore, for the Lawgiver to have legitimate authority in their role as educator they too must be invented and assumed (*OC III*, 381; *CWR Vol. 4*, 154). This is incontrovertible.

According to Rousseau, the tutor must meet certain conditions. The tutor must be well raised themselves. This, of course, raises problems of infinite regress and purpose, because we are left asking who was responsible for raising the tutor and how they did so. Either there a method different to that which Rousseau proposes capable of delivering the results that he desires, or we are left grasping into the past searching for the prime mover of Rousseauian educational practice. Additionally, the tutor must not be employed into the role, they should, in fact, be the child's father. Rousseau writes, "to make a man one must be either a father or more than a man oneself" (*OC IV*, 263; *CWR, Vol. 13*, 176). Not wholly problematic until one considers the third condition that must be met – they must be young. They will be as close in age to Émile as possible. Rousseau writes, "I would want him to be a child himself if it were possible" (*OC IV*, 265; *CWR, Vol. 13*, 177). This is incompatible with both the ideal that the tutor be the father and the requirement that the tutor possess, "the age, health, kinds of knowledge, and all the talent suitable for working at education" (*OC IV*, 264; *CWR, Vol. 13*, 177). Instead of suffering this incoherence, Rousseau assumes this "marvel found" and continues with the project in the hope that, "in considering what he ought to do that we shall see what he ought to be" (*OC IV*, 263; *CWR, Vol. 13*, 176).

This problem is reflected in the Lawgiver who is, in the words of Mark Blackell, "A legislator with an extra-social, quasi-metaphysical source of authority" (2009, 119). It is not simply that one would need "superior intelligence", but one would need faculties so acute that the Lawgiver would see, in Rousseau's words,

> … all men's passions yet experienced none of them; who had no relationship at all to our nature yet knew it thoroughly; whose happiness was independent of us, yet who was nevertheless will to attend to ours; finally one who, preparing for himself a future glory with the passage of time, could work in one century and enjoy the reward in another. Gods would be needed to give men laws.
>
> (*OC III*, 381; *CWR Vol. 4*, 154)

This is not the only concern with Rousseau's figures of authority. Even if they were possible, the type of authority that they possess is troubling. The level of control that they possess extends beyond the application of directive and commands in the fulfilment of their role, to include the active manipulation of those subjects to their authority. This is clearest when considering the authority of God, which for Rousseau plays an instrumental role, and is employed to ensure that the mandates of the General Will are followed by the people who would otherwise not be ready to do so through their own will alone (*OC III*, 383; *CWR Vol. 4*, 156).

In Rousseau's politico-educational project, there is also the authority of oneself. In *The Social Contract*, the tension between the interests of the individual and society reappear within each individual because of their dual role as sovereign citizens and as free individuals. The authority that resides in one's self is thereby in tension because of the sharp separation between the public and private spheres which mirror the roles of Sovereign and free individual. As Sovereign, it is one's responsibility to transcend perceived private interests and act in accordance with the interests of the Republic, whereas in the role of private individual, one retains the freedom and authority to do as one pleases provided that it has no impact on the machinations of the people or the Republic. This can be seen in the difference in freedoms experienced in the state of nature and in civil society. One, in joining in union with others in society, "loses by the social contract … his natural liberty and an unlimited right to everything that tempts him and that he can get" (*OC III*, 364; *CWR, Vol. 4*, 141). However, as Neuhouser notes, where the General Will is silent the individuals of the Republic continue to possess a freedom from interference protected by a set of "established rights" (Neuhouser 2010, 168). Therefore, one retains natural freedom in their private realm in all actions that do not affect the political realm. This is the separation of the public and private realms. However, it is difficult to see how these two worlds remain separate at all times. Furthermore, it is difficult to understand how any one person is able to compartmentalise their roles in society so sharply (Cladis 2007).

Dewey identifies authority as building from communication with others. From this, one can gather that Dewey is attempting to resolve the tension between authority and freedom by justifying authority on different grounds. Dewey seeks to find a resolution by supporting the necessity of authority on the shoulders of experts committed to enquiry. Dewey in effect creates two tiers of authority and participation, two tiers of expert – in the microcosm of society which is the school, there is the student and the teacher, and in society at large, there is the citizen and the public official. It is true that, through the process of communal enquiry, all participants gain authority because they gain knowledge and they continue to reflect upon their values and the values of society. But, these people still have guides and experts that direct and inform them from a position of greater authority. In Dewey's view, it is necessary to employ authority as a tool to place limits on freedom and avoid it degenerating into license (Dewey 1998, 130–31). Legitimate authority is not simply found in these roles however. Dewey is sensitive to the tension between freedom and authority and places a lot of weight on the competence of teachers and public officials in finding the balance between the two forces so that educative growth results from the relationship between teacher and student. As stated above, guidance by the teacher, or other official, should be directed so that their intervention be, "an aid to freedom, not a restriction upon it" (Dewey 1991, 46). However, authority of expertise raises the problem of unjustifiable constraints anew in that the elevation of scientific enquiry to the position of legitimate source of authority may impose upon the freedom of non-experts, thereby compromising Dewey's democratic commitments.

Melvin L. Rogers responds to this concern in his analysis of Dewey's conception of authority and the role that expertise plays within it. It is Rogers' view that according to Dewey, both experts and citizens possess authority, but they do so in different ways. He writes, "Experts come to gain cognitive authority and so become bearers of knowledge because of the audience they address. Citizens are thus authorities just to the extent that it is their problems that create the framework in which expertise functions" (2009, 78). These problems are identified through the deliberation that occurs among the citizens. Deliberation is central to Dewey's conception of legitimate authority. Rogers identifies two points which illustrate the significance of deliberation. First, it is through deliberation that the problems are identified, and it is through deliberation that those identified problems are addressed. As a consequence of this, conflicts are brought out into the open where they can be addressed and understood. Second, deliberation shapes how we come to understand problems and how those problems are contextualised within expert knowledge. Rogers writes, "These two elements suggest that the authority and legitimacy of lay and expert knowledge gains whatever vitality it has from being forged through a deliberative process that makes each responsive to the other" (2009, 79). Therefore, authority justified by expertise persists only in collaboration with the general citizenry. This is consistent with the Deweyan pedagogical practice. The teachers are experts and guide education based upon their observations and interactions with the students under their charge. However, they retain the decision-making power. The teacher, like the public official, is the authority.

There remains, therefore, a risk of the elevation of experts over the general citizenry. This is seen in the two voices of the general citizenry. There is the passive voice which is the, "habitual dimension to the functioning of social life" (Rogers 2009, 82). This requires trust in the existent institutions of that society as a condition of a well-functioning society. Alongside the passive voice, there must be space for an active voice also, one "for sharing in and regulating the uses to which power will be put" (Rogers 2009, 83). However, the scope and weight of the active voice is limited because it is mediated by the experts. Therefore, a tension persists between the experts and the non-experts. To be clear, a tension persists not because experts close the door to an authentic active voice – it is entirely possible that they will not take such oppressive measures – but because of its position as the *de facto* authority.

Therefore, experts, in virtue of this structure, possess within their authority the mechanisms of controlling the active voice which is, as a consequence, under its dominion. A person's freedom is therefore constrained in virtue of the fact that an authority passively persists over them which may silence their active voice arbitrarily. This is inconsistent with Dewey's definition of and commitment to democracy because it reduces Dewey's political philosophy to a defence of two classes of citizen. There persist two classes of citizen even if expertise is more contextual, by which I mean that some people exercise authority in some situations, but less so in others. This is because individuals in certain roles retain authority over others at all times of the relationship in virtue of their role, such as the teacher and public official. Dewey's conception of democracy is built around achieving equal participation (Garrison 1994, 13), but this cannot be attained in a stratified model of citizenship.

Freire's conception of authority is most apparent in the relationship between teacher and student, which in Freire's typology can be expressed in two ways: either as a tension between teacher–student and students–teachers, or as a tension between the revolutionary educator and the oppressed. He writes,

> Through dialogue, the teacher-of-the students and the students-of-the-teacher cease to exist and a new term emerges: teacher-student with students-teachers. The teacher is no longer merely the one-who-teaches, but one who is himself taught in dialogue with the students, who in turn while being taught also teach. They become jointly responsible for a process in which all grow. In this process, arguments based on "authority" are no longer valid; in order to function, authority must be on the side of freedom, not against it.
>
> (2017, 53)

The dialogical conception of authority is in evidence in the proposed reframing of the roles of student and teacher in Freire's problem-posing education. No longer is it the case that the teacher possesses the knowledge and authority in virtue of their role or their expertise; instead, they possess authority through their participation in the dialogical process with their students. They must earn authority. One important aspect of a revolutionary educator earning authority is in their assumption of the role. Freire states the importance of this at various times and always in emphatic language. As noted above, to be a revolutionary educator one must submit to a profound rebirth. They must do this because without the sacrifice, the baggage of assumed knowledge from one's own experience will be imposed upon all new communities. This imposition will be an illegitimate form of authority and an expression of dehumanisation for both the educator and those students subject to the imposition.

Similarly, the students are reformed as students–teachers. The students participate in the learning as they participate in the teaching and the world is transformed by their word. Freire writes, "the teacher-student and the students-teachers reflect simultaneously on themselves and the world without dichotomising this reflection from action, and thus establish an authentic form of thought and action" (2017, 56).

However, there is something deeply troubling about Freire's revolutionary leaders that reminds me of Berlin's concerns of conceptions of positive liberty. In the name of freedom and with egalitarian purpose, they may be unable to overcome the pull of the arrogance of humans. They may reason, as Berlin notes proponents of positive liberty may reason, that they know best and freedom is found along the path that they perceive. Berlin notes that in the name of freedom, "it is easy for me to conceive of myself as coercing others for their own sake, in their, not my, interest. I am then claiming that I know what they truly need better than they know it themselves" (2002, 179). The revolutionary leader may use their own egalitarian intentions and belief in freedom to justify ignoring explicit interests and desires as stated by others, and then claim that the true interests or will of others would align with theirs if they knew better, thereby ignoring the individual's express interest in favour of a hypothetical will that better represents their freedom.

Therefore, it is a delicate balance that Freire's revolutionary leaders are asked to perform. Freire writes, "The leaders do bear the responsibility for co-ordination—and, at times, direction—but leaders who deny praxis to the oppressed thereby invalidate their own praxis" (2017, 99). Jim Walker states that the rebirth which Freire demands of the revolutionary leaders is, "what creates the greatest theoretical difficulties for him, and lays him open to charges of cynical totalitarian elitism, from sophisticated conservatives" (1981, 134). The difficulty leads from Freire's justification of permissible authority. Walker is not the only person to see a problem of authority in Freire's pedagogy. C. A. Bowers argues that the "emancipatory vision" of Freire's pedagogy "is based on the same assumptions that underlie the planetary citizenship envisioned by the neoliberals promoting the Western model of global development" (Bowers and Apffel-Marglin 2005, ix). Peter L. Berger echoes this complaint when he writes,

> ... it is hard to imagine a more 'elitist' program (and, for that matter, a more 'paternalistic' one) than one based on the assumption that a certain group of people is dehumanised to the point of animality, is unable to perceive this condition or rescue itself from it, and requires the (presumably selfless) assistance of others for both the perception and the rescue operation.
>
> (1976, 116)

This tension, which arises in Freire's attempt to explain freedom and its relationship with authority, raises questions about the role of the teacher as revolutionary leader that Freire does not provide an answer to. Regardless of the origin of the revolutionary leader, whether a member of the oppressed in origin or reborn to the side of the oppressed, in entering a community with the aim of freeing people from oppression, questions are raised regarding paternalism and, possibly, elitism. This occurs despite Freire's sensitivity and focus on communication. In fact, it is emphasised as a result of Freire's commitment to class consciousness as a form of privileged knowledge (Freire 1994, 24–27). Ultimately, the demand upon the revolutionary educator is simply too great, they cannot, as any one of us cannot, step outside of their own sphere of knowledge and experience so completely to achieve the Easter experience necessary for the role. What is asked of them is as demanding as any abstract view, any requirement to step outside of oneself, any insular or removed viewpoint imagined in philosophical creativity because they are being asked to assume a particular perspective of privileged knowledge and emerge, not as one with the oppressed, but one of the oppressed – this is a rebirth.

A further worry and connected to the above concern about the practicality of the revolutionary educator is the fact that genuine class suicide, if possible at all, will be indistinguishable from perceived class suicide, which is a manifestation of false generosity. It is a parallel problem to Freire's justification of violence when that violence initiates love (Freire 2017, 30). Nel Noddings comments of Freire's justification of violence, and asks, "What in the history or in the experience of the oppressed leads us to suppose that they will be loving? Or is liberation an act of love simply by virtue of its result?" (1991, 161).[1]

In the case of Rousseau, a tension between authority and freedom persists interactionally in the relationship between authority figures, such as the tutor and the Lawgiver, and those subject to their authority. But it also persists institutionally in the relationship between the private and public realms, and in the relationship between the General Will and the freedom to live as one pleases. In the case of Dewey, the tension between authority and freedom persists in the relationship between experts and non-experts at both interactional and institutional levels, at both levels because citizens effect changes through the participatory democratic conversation and if experts possess an authority over the non-experts, then they do so at the expense of the non-experts' equal voice in both their everyday interactions and in the construct of society, i.e. institutionally. Lastly, as we have just seen, in the case of Freire this tension is not dissolved either. However, if it is possible, it is a problem even more central to Freire than either Rousseau or Dewey.

Freire's pedagogy is explicitly revolutionary. It is its stated aim that the oppressed free themselves from their oppression, an oppression exerted over them by the authority of existing social norms and the people who assume authority in the roles of oppressors. It seeks to challenge and replace existing power relations. As such, one must give an account which can respond to the problems identified within the projects of Rousseau, Dewey, and Freire which persist in the classroom today.

Conclusion

Dewey and Freire attempt what Rousseau was not prepared to do. They took hold of the figurative third rail and sought to explain how, in a political and educational system designed to realise both freedom of the individual and duties towards each other, the authority necessary for its realisation can be present in society and yet does not undermine political and individual freedom. Rousseau ran scared from this problem and hypothesised the characters that led us to our goals, but Dewey and Freire gave us the teachers we need to guide our enquiry and lead us on our path to humanisation. However, in doing so they ran headlong into the very problem that Rousseau sought to avoid – by what means have the teachers and officials postulated by Dewey and Freire achieved their transcendence from corruption and been able to assume the role of expert or leader? We find ourselves asking from where did this authority come, where does it gets its legitimacy, and can this authority be exercised without compromising the process by which we, as a whole, are designed to become uncorrupted and free active agents in both public and private life.

In the following two chapters, I shall seek to gain a greater understanding of what legitimate authority is through an analysis of the concept of authority and how that concept has been explained and implemented in both political and educational contexts. After which I shall apply my new understanding into the methodological foundations provided by Rousseau, Dewey, and Freire. From this position, I will explore a two-pronged resolution to the tension between the individual and society and the problem of authority which I will argue are both equally necessary to overcome the problems encountered in this chapter. As such, the following two chapters will explore the problem of authority from, first, the institutional perspective, and second, from the interactional perspective. This sets the stage for the final two chapters that will form a pair of complementary and mutually co-dependent arguments designed to answer the problem and in turn the tension between the individual and society.

Note

1 I have written about the problems of Freire's educational theory in practice in more detail in "The Incoherence of the Interactional and Institutional Within Freire's Politico-Educational Project" (Wilcock 2020).

References

Berger, Peter L. 1976. *Pyramids of Sacrifice: Political Ethics and Social Change.* New York: Anchor Books.

Berlin, Isaiah. 2002. *Liberty: Incorporating Four Essays on Liberty.* Eds. Henry Hardy and Ian Harris. Oxford: Oxford University Press.

Blackell, Mark. 2009. 'Rousseau, Constant, and the Political Institutionalization of Ambivalence'. In *Rousseau and Desire*, edited by Mark Blackell, John Duncan, and Simon Kow, 117–37. Toronto; Buffalo: University of Toronto Press.

Bowers, C. A., and Frédérique Apffel-Marglin, eds. 2005. *Rethinking Freire: Globalization and the Environmental Crisis*. Sociocultural, Political, and Historical Studies in Education. Mahwah, NJ: Lawrence Erlbaum.

Cladis, Mark Sydney. 2007. *Public Vision, Private Lives: Rousseau, Religion, and 21st-Century Democracy*. New York: Columbia University Press.

Dewey, John. 1976a. 'The School and Society'. In *The Middle Works of John Dewey, 1899–1924, Volume 1: 1899–1901*, edited by Jo Ann Boydston, 1–109. Carbondale: Southern Illinois University Press.

Dewey, John. 1976b. 'The University Elementary School'. In *The Middle Works of John Dewey, 1899–1924, Volume 1: 1899–1901*, edited by Jo Ann Boydston, 317–20. Carbondale: Southern Illinois University Press.

Dewey, John. 1984. 'The Public and Its Problems'. In *The Later Works of John Dewey, 1925–1953, Volume 2: 1925–1927*, edited by Jo Ann Boydston, 235–372. Carbondale: Southern Illinois University Press.

Dewey, John. 1991. 'Experience and Education'. In *The Later Works of John Dewey, 1925–1953. Vol. 13: 1938–1939*, edited by Jo Ann Boydston, 1–62. Carbondale: Southern Illinois University Press.

Dewey, John. 1998. 'Authority and Social Change'. In *The Later Works of John Dewey, 1925–1953: Volume 11: 1935–1937*, edited by Jo Ann Boydston, 130–45. Carbondale: Southern Illinois University Press.

Dewey, John. 2008a. 'Democracy and Education'. In *The Middle Works of John Dewey, 1899–1924, Volume 9: 1916*, edited by Jo Ann Boydston, 1–370. Carbondale: Southern Illinois University Press.

Dewey, John. 2008b. 'Psychological Aspect of the School Curriculum'. In *The Early Works of John Dewey, 1882–1898, Volume 5: 1885–1898*, edited by Jo Ann Boydston, 164–76. Carbondale: Southern Illinois University Press.

Engel, Liba H. 2008. 'Experiments in Democratic Education: Dewey's Lab School and Korczak's Children's Republic'. *The Social Studies* 99 (3): 117–21.

Freire, Paulo. 1978. *Pedagogy in Process: The Letters of Guinea-Bissau*. London: Writers and Readers Publishing Cooperative.

Freire, Paulo. 1984. 'Education, Liberation, and the Church'. *Religious Education* 79 (4): 524–45.

Freire, Paulo. 1994. *Pedagogy of Hope: Reliving Pedagogy of the Oppressed*. Edited by Ana Maria Araújo Freire. New York: Continuum.

Freire, Paulo. 2017. *Pedagogy of the Oppressed*. Translated by Myra Bergman Ramos. London: Penguin Books.

Garrison, Jim W. 1994. 'Realism, Deweyan Pragmatism, and Educational Research'. *Educational Researcher* 23 (1): 5–14.

Hobbes, Thomas. 1988. *Leviathan*. Penguin Classics. Harmondsworth: Penguin Books.

Locke, John. 1980. *Second Treatise of Government*. Indianapolis, IN: Hackett Publishing.

Mayhew, Katherine Camp, and Anna Camp Edwards. 2007. *The Dewey School: The Laboratory School of the University of Chicago 1896–1903*. New York, S.l.: Routledge.

Neuhouser, Frederick. 2010. *Rousseau's Theodicy of Self-Love: Evil, Rationality, and the Drive for Recognition.* Oxford: Oxford University Press.

Noddings, Nel. 1991. *Women and Evil.* Los Angeles, California; London: University of California Press.

Rogers, Melvin L. 2009. 'Democracy, Elites and Power: John Dewey Reconsidered'. *Contemporary Political Theory* 8 (1): 68–89.

Rosenthal, Sandra B. 1986. *Speculative Pragmatism.* Amherst: University of Massachusetts Press.

Rousseau, Jean-Jacques. 1994. *Social Contract; Discourse on the Virtue Most Necessary for a Hero; Political Fragments; and, Geneva Manuscript.* Edited by Roger D. Masters, Christopher Kelly, and Judith R. Bush. The Collected Writings of Rousseau, Vol. 4. Hanover: University Press of New England.

Rousseau, Jean-Jacques. 1999. *Émile. Éducation. Morale. Botanique.* Œuvres Complètes, IV. Paris: Gallimard.

Rousseau, Jean-Jacques. 2003. *Du contrat social. Écrits politiques.* Edited by Bernard Gagnebin and François Bouchardy. Œuvres Complètes, III. Paris: Gallimard.

Rousseau, Jean-Jacques. 2010. *Emile, or, On Education: Includes Émile and Sophie, or, The Solitaries.* Edited by Christopher Kelly. Translated by Allan Bloom. The Collected Writings of Rousseau, Vol. 13. Hanover: University Press of New England.

Schugurensky, Daniel. 2012. 'Citizen School'. In *Paulo Freire Encyclopedia*, edited by Danilo Romeu Streck, 51–53. Lanham, MD: Rowman & Littlefield Publishers.

Walker, Jim. 1981. 'The End of Dialogue: Paulo Freire on Politics and Education'. In *Literacy and Revolution: The Pedagogy of Paulo Freire*, edited by Robert Mackie, 120–50. New York: Continuum.

Wilcock, Neil. 2020. 'The Incoherence of the Interactional and Institutional Within Freire's Politico-Educational Project'. *Studies in Philosophy and Education* 39 (4): 399–414.

Chapter 4

The institutional structure
of education

Introduction

In the preceding chapters, I have established the method that I employ as the foundation for my enquiry using Rousseau, Dewey, and Freire and the commonality between them to pursue an education-centred political project. I have then employed this foundation to identify the end-in-view that I perceive at the heart of a theory of political philosophy that places such import on education. This is the Critical Citizen, a person who is descriptively communitarian, normatively cosmopolitan, an active participant in one's society, and a possessor of both rights and responsibilities. Together, these two preliminary chapters represent the destination and the mode of transport by which we reach it – on the journey itself I have so far remained silent.

In the previous chapter, I began to consider the nature of the obstacles that others have encountered, in particular Rousseau, Dewey, and Freire, in their journey to realise the citizen that they themselves imagined. I identified this as the problem of authority, a recurring problem at the heart of the tension between the individual and society.

At this point, a split occurs in my analysis. I shall, following Rousseau, offer in this and the succeeding chapter two different analyses of the problem of authority. One that focuses on the institutional structures that support and legitimate authority and the second that focuses on the interactional structures that do the same. This separation is a descriptive tool and not a parting of the ways. The interactional and institutional elements of my enquiry are designed to be mutually co-dependent, they stand or fall together, but for the ease of explanation and argumentation, I treat with them separately.

Therefore, in this chapter, I provide an analysis of institutional structures that are designed, at least in part, to support and cultivate the education of the citizen. I do this within the context of the debate on the problem of authority from the previous chapter. Therefore, I shall begin with an exposition of the concept of authority as it has been understood within the political sphere and then contrast that with authority as it manifests and is treated in radical political theory that perceives a great threat in authority.

DOI: 10.4324/9781003271871-5

On top of this analysis, I shall explore models of political structure that seek to offer an answer to the problem of authority and the tension between the interests of the individual and society. Then, I look at models of democratic education that seek to find a balance between the competing interests in cooperative association and those who see the authority of society and the state in schools as something to be prohibited, such as the deschooling movement and the libertarians who advocate for the disestablishment of education and state. Finally, I set out my objections to all of these suggestions in an effort to lay the final pieces into place before I propose the conclusions that I defend.

Authority in the political sphere

Authority can be a nebulous concept. It is something that we feel we understand until we seek to clarify what we mean by its use. We saw in the previous chapter how Rousseau, Dewey, and Freire understood authority and how they attempted to build it into a political model where it did not undermine or compromise freedom, but they are not alone in this endeavour. Political philosophers have continually sought to uncover the definition, source, and ontology of legitimate authority. Hannah Arendt is responsible for one of the most influential and considered expositions of authority. According to Arendt, authority has been lost due to its equivocation with violence, which results from a tendency to relate everything to a functional context. Therefore, authority becomes everything which makes people obey (Arendt 1993, 91). This can be seen as a response to those who maintain that authority contains elements of power and force within it. People like Charles W. Hendel who writes,

> Power is, ... , an essential element of authority, and authority is a sustaining power for the whole community. It asserts the claim of the community upon the lives and conduct of those who are part of it, and asserts it on occasion by applying it with force.
>
> (1958, 13)

Arendt defines authority, in very Rousseauian terms, as the, "unquestioning recognition by those who are asked to obey; neither coercion nor persuasion is needed" (1970, 45). Arendt argues that, when an authority issues a command of a subject, they are giving a reason for following that command, namely, that it has been issued by a recognised authority. I shall circle back to what constitutes a recognised authority shortly; however, first it is important to note that there is no other consideration for those subject to authority. The command, in coming from a recognised authority, is not to be understood as an additional reason for following a command. It does not stack onto other reasons which supports the command, because, for Arendt, authority does not require reasons. Authority is distinct from persuasion and is identifiable as the following of a command without argument or force.

Furthermore, for Arendt, it is not the case that authority may strategically employ persuasion, or coercive force, in order to reassert itself. She writes,

> ... authority precludes the use of external means of coercion; where force is used, authority itself has failed. Authority, on the other hand, is incompatible with persuasion, which presupposes equality and works through a process of argumentation. Where arguments are used, authority is left in abeyance.
>
> (1993, 93)

According to the definition of authority given by Arendt, a person who employs persuasion or force, whether they possessed authority or not, would be expressing a different quality in doing so. For example, an expression of coercive force is one of violence not authority, and whilst a violent command is effective in accomplishing compliance, that compliance is not related to authority. Arendt writes, "Out of the barrel of a gun grows the most effective command, resulting in the most instant and perfect obedience. What never can grow out of it is power" (1970, 53). Violence and authority are distinct from one another, as is persuasion.

What constitutes a recognised authority according to Arendt is found in social and institutional relationships. Arendt writes that authority,

> ... can be vested in persons – there is such a thing as personal authority, as, for instance, in the relation between parent and child, between teacher and pupil – or it can be vested in offices, as, for instance, in the Roman senate (*auctoritas in senatu*) or in the hierarchical offices of the Church (a priest can grant valid absolution even though he is drunk).
>
> (1970, 45)

Therefore, in Arendt's conception of authority, there is a particular focus on tradition as the source of authority and it is in the loss of our attachment to certain traditions that results in her view that authority has been replaced by power, violence, and persuasion masquerading under its name. However, there is, in the appeal to the authority held by offices, a commitment to the legitimacy of authority that is supported by the law, whether that be the law of the church or the state.

Carl J. Friedrich shares much of Arendt's understanding of authority. Where they differ is mostly found in where they identify the source of authority. Unlike Arendt, Friedrich does not place authority in the person but in that person's ability to communicate. This is an important distinction because it means that it is not in virtue of being a parent that one has authority over their child, nor is it in virtue of being the Prime Minister of a country that one has authority over that country's citizens. Furthermore, it attempts to answer the complication of the reasons behind a command being considered a part of the reasons to follow that command. Friedrich explains,

> ... when I speak of authority, I wish to say that the communications of a person possessing it exhibits a very particular kind of relationship to reason and reasoning. Such communication, whether opinions or commands, are not demonstrated through rational discourse, but they possess the potentiality of reasoned deliberation – they are 'worthy of acceptance.'
>
> (1958, 35)

In accordance with this view, Friedrich claims that in any utterance of authority, there are reasons that support that utterance, but these reasons are not expressed in the communication of that utterance, they exist in potentiality. These reasons can, in theory, be called forth and made explicit because the authority of a person rests in their "capacity to issue authoritative communications" (Friedrich 1958, 36). Furthermore, these communications hold weight only when they are "based upon reasoning that has meaning not only to X, but also to A, B, and C, in the sense of being related to knowledge which they all possess, or to opinions, beliefs, and values which they all share" (Friedrich 1958, 36). This distinction aims to avoid importing persuasion into a working definition of authority, and it aims to explain how neither the superordinate or subordinate in an authority relation suspend their reason as they do their judgement.

Therefore, a person who possesses authority in their communication does so because of their shared values with the people who are subject to their authoritative communications and their capacity for reasoned deliberation. Without this capacity, there can be no genuine authority (Friedrich 1958, 37). The difference between Arendt and Friedrich is in the role of reasons. For Arendt, the only reason necessary is – because the command is issued by a recognised authority. This is not sufficient according to Friedrich, according to whom it is necessary that there be reasons that support that command although they need not be spoken. It is Arendt's view that with the breakdown of tradition and religion as the source of authority that authority itself has been all but lost. What is spoken of as authority is in fact power or coercion (Arendt 1993, 1956), whereas Friedrich offers a positive argument based around his notion of reasoned elaboration.

The sociologist Max Weber offers a further similar understanding of authority to Arendt and Friedrich but differs, again, mostly in the understanding of the source of authority. Weber identifies three different types of legitimate authority: legal–rational authority, traditional authority, and charismatic authority. With respect to the first two, Weber's conception of authority can be seen as mirroring Arendt. Legal–rational authority, on Weber's view, is found in the belief that commands and regulations expressed by the law and by those who embody the law are expressed by right. It is explained by a belief in the legitimacy and validity of the rule of law. In legal–rational authority, the locus of authority is in a set of rules or principles formalised and codified. Therefore, legal–rational authority demands that one follow the dictates of the person who fills the role which bears authority granted by those principles. Peter M. Blau writes in his analysis of Weber's theory of authority, "the assumption is that a body of legal rules has been deliberately established to further the rational pursuit of collective goals" (1963, 308).

Weber's idea of traditional authority is supported by a person's belief, "in the sanctity of immemorial traditions and the legitimacy of those exercising authority under them" (Weber 1978, 215). It is that which is vested in a person or institution in virtue of a faith in the long-standing traditions that established and supported those institutions and the people expressing authority from their position within that institution. Traditional authority transcends any one particular person or role; it is attached to the belief in the legitimacy of that authority expressed over time. Blau encapsulates the notion of traditional authority in the statement, "The King is dead – long live the King" (1963, 308).

Charismatic authority is something different. It resides in a person due to their particular, "sanctity, heroism or exemplary character" (Weber 1978, 215). In this instance, the person would hold authority regardless of whether they held any social or institutional relationship. Blau notes that charismatic authority, "usually acts as a revolutionary force" (1963, 308). According to Weber, all three of these sources of authority can be legitimate.

The alternative and the radical

A different approach to that taken by Arendt, Friedrich, and Weber towards understanding the complexity of the concept of authority is found in rights-based accounts like those of Joseph Raz, who is, at least in part, responding directly to R. P. Wolff's definition and categorisation of authority in opposition to freedom. According to Wolff, "Authority is the right to command, and correlatively, the right to be obeyed" (1998, 4). Wolff draws the sharpest separation possible between authority and autonomy. He writes that autonomy is, "a combination of freedom and responsibility; it is a submission to laws which one has made for oneself" (1998, 14). As such, one is not subject to any person's will besides their own. Wolff goes on to argue that any instance of authority, if heeded, is an unjustifiable constraint on a person's freedom and therefore is incompatible with autonomy, and that, "philosophical anarchism would seem to be the only reasonable political belief for an enlightened man" (Wolff 1998, 19). In commentating on Wolff's framing of the tension between authority and autonomy, David Miller writes,

> According to Wolff it shows that the idea of a *de jure* or legitimate authority is a contradiction in terms. There are no circumstances in which I should recognise an obligation to obey somebody simply because he has commanded it, because in doing so I would be breaching my primary obligation to be autonomous.
>
> (1984, 26–27)

Raz does not challenge Wolff's definitions of authority or autonomy but instead offers three theses which together are designed to resist the conclusion that they are incompatible (Raz 1990b, 2009b; 2009a). Together, these theses form the service conception of authority which argues that the source of a person's or institution's authority is based on the judgement of the subject of that authority. It is Raz's view that, the primary reason for a subject to recognise them as a legitimate authority is whether there is sufficient evidence,

> ... that the alleged subject is likely better to comply with reasons which apply to him ... if he accepts the directives of the alleged authority as authoritatively binding and tries to follow them, rather than by trying to follow the reasons which apply to him directly.
>
> (Raz 2009b, 129)

In other words, the object of authority is adjudged to possess authority because it is better to follow that authority than strike out independently of it. Raz refers to this as the normal justification thesis. It is a minimal commitment to the authority of reason which leads the subject to succumb to the epistemic authority of the object's greater rational judgement.

The normal justification thesis is supported by the dependence thesis which states that, "All authoritative directives should be based, in the main, on reasons which already independently apply to the subjects of the directives and are relevant to their action in the circumstances covered by the directive" (Raz 1990b, 125). This condition of legitimate authority aims to address concerns of arbitrary expressions of authority that extend beyond the scope of that authority and the interests of those commanded.

The pre-emptive thesis follows from the dependence thesis. Raz writes,

> The fact that an authority requires performance of an action is a reason for its performance which is not to be added to all other relevant reasons when assessing what to do, but should exclude and take the place of some of them.
>
> (1990b, 124)

This is different to Arendt and Friedrich who argue that the command of a recognised authority does not provide additional reasons for following that command; it *is* the reason to follow that command. Raz is proposing that the command operates independently of individual reasons and overrides some of those reasons. Scott Hershovitz notes that for Raz authoritative orders are compound, "they are both first-order reasons to act as the order requires and second-order exclusionary reasons not to act on (at least some) countervailing considerations" (Hershovitz 2011, 3–4). The dependence, pre-emptive, and normal justification theses, together, are Raz's service conception of authority (Raz 1990b, 131).

According to Hershovitz though, the service conception of authority is not an adequate model of legitimate authority. One reason for this is that it fails to capture the conditions of political authority because the scope of political authorities is more broad than the capacity to guide the reason of those subject to it. This is a procedural objection because the service conception of authority applies beyond the political realm, to interactional relationships also. However, in its generality, it does not recognise any special claims for obedience by those subject to the authority of the democratic state. This is not a problem for Raz and he states that the service conception of authority is intentionally not couched in democratic terms because democratic regimes may not be legitimate (Raz 2006, 1031 ftn. 20).

A problem that arises for Raz as a result is that there is no clear way to identify between authority claims when more than one person fulfils the criteria at any one time. Hershovitz notes that, "If several people are able to play a role, we need a method of choosing among them" (2011, 12). Furthermore, it seems that the service conception of authority is counterintuitive to how we understand authority relations in everyday life. Hershovitz writes, "It is not clear that the normal justification thesis can account for the fact that children are subject to the authority of their parents, not to the authority of all those who could parent well" (2011, 12). Further to this, of course, is that a child may have parents that parent poorly, but to a minimum standard where their authority over the child is not challenged by institutions of the state. There is no other adult that is able to trump their authority regardless of their competency or superior directives.

I do not believe that Hershovitz's objection to the service conception of authority is successful because it assumes that our existing common practices with respect to authority hold some normative power. It is certainly the case that I have no authority to parent another person's child, even when that child is being neglected or abused but there certainly are mechanisms in place, such as social services and safeguarding obligations, that aim to address this, sometimes counterintuitive, limitation of the authority of third parties. The service conception of authority seeks to capture an idea of legitimate authority that is not limited by the institutions that govern us, and it will generate some counterintuitive examples of legitimate authority but that does not necessarily refute their legitimacy.

This being said, it is unclear that Raz has successfully overcome the problem established by Wolff. In accepting Wolff's definitions of authority and autonomy and seeking to make them compatible, Raz risks trivialising one or the other. This triviality is suggested when Raz writes, "Surely what counts, from the point of view of the person in authority, it is not what the subject thinks but how he acts" (1990b, 119). This statement appears to trivialise freedom because it matters not how the person subject to a command has come to their decision to act in accordance with it. What matters is that they have acted in accordance with that command and therefore been subject to authority. Raz appears to run roughshod over coinciding reasons and those implicit reasons which inform the nature of one's compliance. In contrast, according to Wolff, the autonomous person is not subject to any person's will besides their own, and while they may act in accordance with the commands or will of another, they do so, "not *because* he has been told to do it" (Wolff 1998, 14). It is in this way that a person can satisfy the conditions of being politically free. Further to this, Wolff claims that the authority of the subject and the actions of the object can come apart, and what matters is not a person's action with respect to commands received by an authority but the intention behind that action. In Wolff's words, "my complying with his command does not constitute an acknowledgment on my part of any such authority" (Wolff 1998, 6).

These two seemingly divergent views on authority can in fact be consistent with one another because they issue from differing perspectives of the equation. One looking as it does from the object of authority and the other from the viewpoint of those subject to that authority. However, the spirit of these two claims is wholly inconsistent with one another and raises serious questions about the ontology of authority, questions that I will return to when I consider the relationship between the two or more people in an authority relation in Chapter 5.

What is clear is that R. P. Wolff acts as the lightning rod of the anarchist critique of authority. Joseph Raz writes in the introduction to his edited collection of essays on the justification of authority, that, "No one has brought out the problematic aspect of authority better than Robert Paul Wolff in his *In Defense of Anarchism*" (1990a, 3). However, while it is true that anarchists reject authority and phrase this rejection in strong terms, Wolff's philosophical anarchism takes a hard line which most anarchists would not draw. Authority persists in anarchist theory.

It is easy to find instances of the anarchist rejecting authority. The anarchist theorist and biographer George Woodcock notes that Sébastian Faure wrote, "Whoever denies authority and fights against it is an anarchist" (Woodcock 1963, 7). In *The Conquest of Bread*, Peter Kropotkin wrote that an Anarchist–Communist society is one that, "recognises the absolute liberty of the individual, that does not admit of any authority, and makes use of no compulsion to drive men to work" (Kropotkin 1995, 128). Mikhail Bakunin wrote that "We are in fact enemies of all authority, for we realise that power and authority corrupt those who exercise them as much as those who are compelled to submit to them" (1964, 249). Errico Malatesta defined anarchy as, "society organised without authority" and states that, "authority not only is not necessary for social organisation but, far from benefitting it, lives on it parasitically, hampers its development and uses its advantages for the special benefit of a particular class which exploits and oppresses the others" (2015, 14). Lastly, Peter H. Marshall quotes a similarly anti-authoritarian statement by Colin Ward who called an anarchist society, "a society which organises itself without authority" (1993, 42). However, Marshall cautions against the simplicity of statements such as these. He writes,

> Authority is more fundamental and exists prior to the foundation of the State. In addition, it might be misleading to define anarchy as an absence of authority for strictly speaking it would appear that a society without some form of authority is virtually inconceivable.
>
> (1993, 42)

Similarly, Judith Suissa, in her analysis of authority in anarchist theory, argues that, "It is ... not logically inconceivable that a political system calling itself a state could be compatible with anarchist principles" (2011, 56). This is because the objections to the state that the anarchist employs are directed to a particular construct of that state and not the state in and of itself. Therefore, Suissa argues that the objection to the state by the anarchist is instrumental rather than intrinsic. Furthermore, even if the anarchist was committed to the absolute rejection of the state, it does not necessarily follow that the anarchist is committed to the absolute rejection of authority. Suissa references Richard T. De George, "who argues that most anarchist theorists were well aware of the fact that some kind of authority is necessary for social organisation to function" (Suissa 2011, 58).

So how does the anarchist perceive the form of legitimate authority? De George reformulates the rejection of authority by the anarchist as the rejection of a top–down model of authority, where authority is imposed upon the individual from above. De George refers to this as authoritarianism. He writes, "Authoritarianism starts at the top and directs those below for the benefit of those above" (1978, 98). Legitimate authority for the anarchist, De George explains, is that which originates from the people themselves and is directed across society. He continues,

> If authority is to be compatible with anarchism it must start from below, be constantly responsive to its source, and be used for the benefit of the people subject to it. The root problem is to provide organisation without authoritarianism.
>
> (1978, 98)

Examples of this according to De George, are epistemic authority and authority of competence. In this way, legitimate authority is expressed as a hypothetical imperative. For these reasons, it must be noted that the radical rejection of authority is often a qualified rejection.

It may be unclear whether the anarchist theorist is successful in offering an account of authority which does not undermine their commitment to anarchism. However, what is clear is that whether authority is perceived as a threat to freedom, as in the case of the anarchist and those sympathetic with the anarchist suspicion of authority, or whether it is perceived as the root of stable government as is argued by Raz, Arendt, Friedrich, and Weber, it is recognised that there is a tension between authority and freedom, and a tension between authority and reason. The concept of authority that is being developed on both sides of the equation is representative of a commitment to find a coherent expression of authority with freedom and reason.

The institutional response of democratic education

We have seen that Rousseau, Dewey, and Freire each addressed the tension between the individual and society and the problem of authority with models of democratic education. While not the dominant political approach, it is one that continues most notably in the work of Amy Gutmann, whose conceptualisation of democratic education is arguably the most significant contribution to the discussion since Dewey's *Democracy and Education*. Nancy Rosenblum writes of *Democratic Education*, "It is more than just another contribution to the genre of philosophy and public affairs. *Democratic Education* is exemplary" (1988, 1355).

The education advocated by Gutmann aims to cultivate democratic virtues and a, "conscious social reproduction," which she identifies as, "the ways in which citizens are or should be empowered to influence the education that in turn shapes the political values, attitudes, and modes of behaviour of future citizens" (Gutmann 1999, 14). Gutmann does not give an exhaustive list of what the democratic virtues are that she imagines will result from this education process, and nor would she want to, because the function of conscious social reproduction is to permit change over time. In *Democratic Education*, Gutmann defines democratic virtue as, "the ability to deliberate, and hence to participate in conscious social reproduction" (1999, 46). At another point, Gutmann states that democratic virtue includes, "the willingness and ability of citizens to reason collectively and critically about politics" (1999, 107). Then again as toleration, truth-telling, and a predisposition to non-violence (Gutmann 1999, 173). However, it is important to note that the virtues of the democratic character, according to Gutmann, are equivalent to the deliberative character (Gutmann 1999, 51). In an interview conducted as a part of a larger reflection on *Democratic Education* thirty years after its initial publication, Gutmann was asked what constitutes deliberative character, she responded,

> The cultivation of truth-seeking and truth-telling, tolerance and mutual respect, the skills and virtues of robust yet reasoned debate, a willingness to forge and support beneficial compromises in decision-making, and a basic understanding of the value of deliberation – as well as its limits – all are keys to improving pluralist democratic societies.
>
> (Quoted in Sardoc 2018, 248)

Gutmann's model of democratic education and the citizen that inhabits it is a prominent but not singular attempt to define the desirable form of the citizen. For example, in tension with Gutmann's argument, Stephen G. Gilles argues in favour of the priority of parental rights over the authority of the state and their children in determining the values that ought to be inculcated in the next generation (Gilles 1996); William Galston argues that the state is obligated to ensure that every person receives a "basic civic education", which he defines as, "the beliefs and habits that support the polity and enable individuals to function competently in public affairs" (1991, 252); Meira Levinson notes that what constitutes the necessary set of civic skills and attitudes of an individual is dependent, to some degree, on their culture, heritage, community, and socio-economic background (Levinson 2014); and Eamonn Callan promotes what he calls "liberal soulcraft", ordinarily associated with conservatism, soulcraft is, "the moulding of citizens according to some traditional standard of human excellence" (2010, 5). Despite the differences between these models of citizenship and democratic education, they are each firmly placed within the tradition of civic education which aims to educate its members to develop the values, virtues, and mindset of existing societal norms, albeit, in most cases, with the scope for limited change.

These examples are all instances of political and educational theory. A clear practical example of democratic education that is representative of a comparable approach can be seen in the United Kingdom since the publication of *The Crick Report* in 1998 and the introduction of compulsory citizenship education in England and Wales. The stated aim and purpose of *The Crick Report* is to make secure and to increase the knowledge, skills, and values relevant to the nature and practice of participatory democracy; also to enhance the awareness of rights and duties, and the sense of responsibilities needed for the development of pupils into active citizens; and in so doing, to establish the value to individuals, schools, and society or involvement in the local and wider community (*The Crick Report* 1998, 40). Further to this, the report states that an understanding of the democratic apparatus and the bodies of the democratic state is necessary to perceive the relationship between political activity and civil society and, "to cultivate awareness and concern for world affairs and global issues" (*The Crick Report* 1998, 40).

There are three educational strands of *The Crick Report*, together they are designed to develop the Crickian citizen. There is social and moral responsibility, which constitutes the learning of, "self-confidence and socially and morally responsible behaviour … towards those in authority and towards each other"; community involvement, which involves learning about and becoming involved in one's local community; and political literacy, a term at the heart of Crick's political theory which is described in *The Crick Report* as, "Pupils learning about and how to make themselves effective in public life through knowledge, skills and values" (*The Crick Report* 1998, 40–41).

The citizen of *The Crick Report* is designed to find the balance between rights and responsibilities and is also designed to be an active member of their community both politically and socially. In *The Crick Report*, there are seventeen essential values and dispositions to be cultivated as a part of one's education. These include, concern for the common good, belief in human dignity and equality, concern to resolve conflicts, practice of tolerance, courage to defend a point of view, determination to act justly, commitment to active citizenship, and concern for human rights. Together, they represent the "democratic virtues" and while many, or maybe all, of these values and dispositions seem uncontroversial in themselves, accompanied by the stated aim of common citizenship, they become significantly narrower in scope and the context in which they are held is a cause for concern because they fail to respect the politics of difference.

Despite the fact that *The Crick Report* clearly aims to be inclusive, it is written in a language which treats groups outside of the dominant culture of the United Kingdom as other. Mark Olssen addresses this concern within *The Crick Report*. He writes,

> In *The Crick Report* there is the notion of a single national identity to which all is referred and to which citizenship education aspires. It is argued throughout the Report that certain uniform conceptions of moral values and social development constitute an essential precondition for citizenship.
>
> (2004, 180)

In addition to its explicit statement, the argument in favour of a shared identity is also implied throughout *The Crick Report*, transforming the citizen into an insidious construct. Terence H. McLaughlin draws attention to objections to *The Crick Report* of this manner (McLaughlin 2000). It is claimed that *The Crick Report* possesses, "an illicit bias in relation to particular substantive matters … through omission" (McLaughlin 2000, 552). While the report states its intention as developing a model of citizenship and citizenship education which is "sensitive to ethnic diversity" (*The Crick Report* 1998, 17) and which respects cultural differences between groups, the language used elsewhere in the report betrays a more assimilationist attitude. Osler and Starkey write that, "the report ... falls into the trap of presenting certain ethnicities as 'other' when it discusses cultural diversity" (2001, 292). This view of ethnic minorities is most apparent when it is stated in the report that, "minorities must learn to respect the laws, codes and conventions as much as the majority—not merely because it is useful to do so, but because this process helps foster common citizenship" (*The Crick Report* 1998, 18). This is the language of assimilation and integration and, in virtue of the fact that *The Crick Report* intends to mould each generation through education, it is a worrying example of the primacy of authority over freedom. As a result, *The Crick Report* is noted for failing to respect the politics of difference (Olssen 2004, 181).

In representing those outside of the dominant culture as "other," *The Crick Report* contains within it a latent racism, and in the words of Olssen, "represents the white British as the majority who must learn to tolerate minorities" (Olssen 2004, 182). Furthermore, in speaking of a common citizenship which minorities must make additional effort to subscribe to shows too little respect for the conventions of those outside of the dominant culture and is expressive of a colonial attitude. The report of *The Commission on the Future of Multi-Ethnic Britain*, commonly referred to as the Parekh Report, directly addresses these ignored issues of citizenship and multiculturalism and is critical of *The Crick Report* for its insidious othering of people outside of the dominant cultural group. It recognises that citizens are both individuals and members of groups. The report states, "Britain is both a community of citizens and a community of communities, both a liberal and a multicultural society, and needs to reconcile their sometimes conflicting requirements" (*The Parekh Report* 2006, ix). In extension of this objection to *The Crick Report*, similar concerns have been expressed regarding the attitude towards gender contained within the report (Arnot et al. 2000; Phillips 2000).

In opposition to democratic education

A significant concern with these models of democratic education is that the set of values highlighted as desirable and cultivated through education is that they represent the values of existing dominant power relations, in particular the authority of the state and the values that continue a state-like-this. They are models that do not permit or encourage much deviation from how things are now and are, therefore, models of self-preservation. This is an extension of the objection to *The Crick Report* above. It is not only the marginalised that find themselves tolerated and expected to conform but all people whose values differ from the values that uphold the existing state of affairs.

Michael W. McConnell argues that there can be no set of values that constitutes the democratic citizen that does not fall to controversy. According to McConnell, there is a myriad of competing thick concepts of democratic values and that imposition of any one of these, "contradicts the premise of a liberal pluralistic society: that there be no official orthodoxy" (McConnell 2002, 102). Further to this, McConnell argues that one may be able to defend a thin conception of the democratic citizen; however, in order to find agreement, one would lose the meaningfulness of the conception and by extension the appeal of its construction. McConnell writes, "there is no set of agreed-upon values for democratic citizens, except perhaps at a level of vagueness that ceases to be controversial because it ceases to be meaningful" (2002, 101).

Arguments of this sort, which pick as their target the influence of the state in the development of persons through the schooling system, intend to show that values that are supported by the state are necessarily coercive in nature and an unjustified limitation of freedom. In particular, potentially controversial areas of study, like citizenship, religion, and sex and relationship education are the focus of the conversation. However, it is not just defenders of a radical individualism like the libertarianism of Milton Freidman (1955) and Michael W. McConnell (2002) but also defenders of a radical egalitarianism like Ivan Illich (2000) and Everett Reimer (1971) who seek to show the coercive force of state-mandated and controlled education. I will introduce both approaches in turn.

The view that the influence of the state in education must be constrained and subordinated in the name of freedom where that freedom supports a radical individualism underpins the defence of basic civic education or a civic minimum. Which promotes the teaching of only those values that are uncontroversial or that everyone can agree on. Milton Freidman addressed this issue and argued that in, "a free private enterprise exchange economy, government's primary role is to preserve the rules of the game by enforcing contracts, preventing coercion, and keeping markets free" (1955, 123). Friedman argues that state-mandated and financed education is justified on account of the mutual benefit of all persons in the education of the next and each subsequent generation. However, Friedman resists the next step in the state education argument, the justification of the, "actual administration of educational institutions by the government, the 'nationalisation', as it were, of the bulk of the 'education industry'" (Freidman 1955, 126). In its place, Friedman proposes publicly funded private education through the distribution of vouchers to parents so that they can exercise their freedom and choose where to send their child to school. A number of people have taken up Friedman's mantle and, in the USA at least, the conversation between publicly funded and controlled and publicly funded private education continues.

Another advocate of publicly funded private education is Michael W. McConnell who argues that a model of civic minimalism can represent the values of a pluralistic society better than democratic education. He argues that a model of democratic education either aims to inculcate in the next generation, "values that have been adopted, in fact, by the people through democratic processes", which he refers to as democratically derived values; or it aims to inculcate the values that are necessary for the development and stability of a democratic society, this he refers to as substantively democratic values (McConnell 2002, 98).

McConnell's objection to substantively democratic values is clear. He believes that there would be a myriad of competing thick concepts of democratic values and that if one was supported by state education then those values would be unjustifiably imposed on those who live by different values. Implementation of any one thick conception runs contrary to the foundational premise of the liberal pluralistic society by imposing a fixed set of values on its people. Therefore, it is only possible to support a thin approach to substantively democratic values. He writes, "Certain values and virtues are essential to a democratic society, but they are relatively few and they are subject to many different interpretations" (McConnell 2002, 102).

In the case of democratically derived values, McConnell argues that families are better placed than the state to choose the content of the values inculcated through schooling, "just as we allow them to choose their own religion" (2002, 99). This is because, so McConnell argues, democratic education cannot accommodate the interests of those who see religious faith as essential in the education of their children. McConnell writes, "The objective of social reproduction is to reproduce, in the next generation, the set of values and beliefs that constitute the character of society" (2002, 101). If that is so, he goes on to argue, then the parents and local communities are better placed to achieve this aim representing, as they do, the embodiment of the values that they wish to continue. Therefore, McConnell advocates the disestablishment of education and state in the same way that the church is separate from schooling.

A similar concern with compulsory education arises in the deschooling movement by authors such as Illich and Reimer. Illich argues that education inhibits learning. He writes, "for most men the right to learn is curtailed by the obligation to attend school" (2000, vii). This is because, according to Illich, it is impossible to provide universal equal education in any meaningful way and therefore schooling encourages social stratification because people are valued not for their learning but for their schooling. Illich perceives a conflation between the process of going through an education and the substance of that which has been learned. A "schooled" society will value the person who has received more process and not consider the substance of that which has been learned through that process. It is for this reason that Illich argues society, not just education but society as a whole, must be deschooled. It is important to note that Illich's views changed significantly over time, but I shall focus on the arguments within his book *Deschooling Society*.

This view is shared by Reimer who argues that school, in the extended sense to mean all educational institutions, is a system of continued oppression and widening inequality. It is a place which, regardless of intention, suits the interests of the wealthy and powerful, not the poor. Both Illich and Reimer use the word "school" in this extended sense and Illich appears to use the word "schooled" to convey the meaning of insidious training or belief. According to Illich, within school, the students are "schooled" to conflate the meanings of a variety of different concepts, most notably "process" and "substance".

The confusion leads to the belief that there is a direct correlation between participating in and progressing through "schooling" and education, and the depth and meaning of one's knowledge. Illich believes this confusion goes further, "The pupil," he writes, "is 'schooled' to confuse teaching with learning, grade advancement with education, a diploma with competence, and fluency with the ability to say something new" (2000, 1). Similarly, Reimer argues that,

> School has become the universal church of a technological society, incorporating and transmitting its ideology, shaping men's minds to accept this ideology, and conferring social status in proportion to its acceptance. There is no question of man's rejecting technology. The question is only one of adaptation, direction and control.
>
> (1971, 19)

This view of schooling that Illich and Reimer describe cements existing power relations because, regardless of the money spent on the education of the poor, equality will not result, but the belief that the poor have been given that opportunity will serve to further the myth that education is the tool to achieve equality. Both Illich and Reimer employ empirical evidence to support their arguments. They reference evidence that money invested into education struggles to ever reach the children intended (Illich 2000, 127–35). Reimer, writing in 1970, notes that,

> The children in the poorest one-tenth of the United States population attend school for an average of less than five years. The schools they attend, at this grade level, spend no more than $500 per pupil per year. These children cost the public, in schooling, less than $2,500 each over a lifetime. The children of the richest one-tenth of the population finish college and a year of graduate school, which costs about $35,000. Assuming that one-third of this is private expenditure, the richest one-tenth still get ten times as much public finds for education as the poorest one-tenth.
>
> (1971, 128)

Now, while these figures will no longer be accurate, the general argument contained within them is. It is still the case that for the most part those people that go no further in education than the compulsory minimum are disproportionately from the poorest backgrounds. While those people that progress to higher education are disproportionately from wealthier backgrounds. Therefore, those people are receiving a greater benefit from government investment in education, and therefore, it is not an equalising power.

Educational opportunities cannot, according to Illich, be remedied in the schooling environment because those opportunities exist in the lifestyle difference between the rich and the poor (Illich 2000, 6). Whereas Reimer states that, "Schools constitute a regressive tax because the privileged go to school longer and because costs increase with the level of schooling" (1971, 129). Illich and Reimer go further; however, as Herbert Gintis notes, for Illich, "The institutionalisation of values occurs not through external coercion, but through psychic manipulation, so its rejection is an apolitical act of individual will. The movement for social change thus becomes a cultural one of raising consciousness" (Gintis 1972, 74). In a similar vein, Reimer astutely observes that it is not only the financial funding that is prohibitive to the poorest students. It is not simply that the poor are not receiving the benefits, but they are subject to continued manipulation and psychological imprisonment by schooling. He writes,

> ... the poor suffer the handicap of the culture of silence, the inheritance of magic and myth designed to ensure their continued docility. It is this, rather than deficient genes, which handicaps the learning of their children; this plus the punishment of failure and disapproval which is their customary lot in schools. ... If all of the public funds allotted to education in every nation were spent exclusively upon the poor it would still take many generations to offset the handicaps which generations of exploitation have imposed upon them.
>
> (1971, 130)

According to Illich, even for the poor, most of their learning occurs outside of the classroom. He writes, "Most learning happens casually, and even most intentional learning is not the result of programmed instruction" (2000, 12). To support this claim, Illich draws on some very persuasive examples: the learning of one's mother tongue, the learning of a second language, the learning of reading – these according to Illich are all examples of learning more effectively done casually and through the circumstances of life that bring us to them and not in the school environment. Reimer, on the other hand, argues that because the people that most need the resources that education financing pays for are not the recipients of the benefits those resources incur, we cannot justifiably finance education by funding schooling publicly (Reimer 1971, 128).

Illich challenges the idea that education for all can be provided. In its place, Illich defends voluntary learning webs. He writes, "The most radical alternative to school would be a network or service which gave each man the same opportunity to share his current concern with others motivated by the same concern" (2000, 19). The idea behind these learning webs, is that the authority of the individual is found not in their title, job, or place in social hierarchy but by their effective participation in disestablished learning.

In contrast, Reimer defends distributing a kind of educational welfare where the recipients receive the monetary value directly. However, neither Illich nor Reimer pay sufficient attention to the coercive nature of the economy. As Gintis notes, "Illich's Good Society is based on small scale entrepreneurial (as opposed to corporate) capitalism, with perfectly competitive markets in goods and services" (Gintis 1972, 75). Similarly, Reimer maintains an important place for the market and even though he recognises that, "Charlatans and profiteers might have a field day for a time," he maintains a faith that a balance would be achieved. He writes, "Controls of the type offered by better business bureaus would be sufficient, since they would be too inefficient to do much harm but available for use against a real mountebank" (Reimer 1971, 135).

Conclusion

The concern of both the libertarian and the radical egalitarian is with how the authority of the state is expressed through a state-funded and controlled education system. The impact of which is a clear manifestation of the tension between the individual and society. In the eyes of the libertarian, this is the interest of the state in cultivating an image of a particular model of the citizen, putting pressure on the interest of the individual and their community to cultivate the next generation to hold the values of that individual and community. In the eyes of the radical egalitarian, it is a more direct concern of the coercion involved in a state imposing a value system that is designed to perpetuate the existing state of affairs and power relations by shaping the minds of the next generation. This is seen simply as an unjustifiable constraint upon the interests of the individual. However, it must be noted that the models of democratic education discussed in this chapter are not naïve to this tension. They are aware of it and they seek to redress it by capturing a value system that supports the citizenry in their collective endeavour, but in doing so, they trade off interests of the individual for the wellbeing and stability of that collective.

I will end the discussion of the relationship between authority and the institutional structure of education here, and I will return to it when I answer the problem with my own position that I believe addresses the problems that I have raised. This will be the subject of Chapter 6, but first I shall shift the discussion from the institutional to the interactional and look again at the problem of authority but with a focus on how it manifests in our relationships with each other, especially within the education setting.

References

Arendt, Hannah. 1956. 'Authority in the Twentieth Century'. *The Review of Politics* 18 (4): 403–17.

Arendt, Hannah. 1970. *On Violence*. New York: Harcourt, Brace & World.

Arendt, Hannah. 1993. 'What Is Authority?' In *Between Past and Future: Eight Exercises in Political Thought*, 91–141. New York: Penguin Books.

Arnot, Madeleine, Helena Araújo, Kiki Deliyanna-Kouimtzis, Gabrielle Ivinson, and Amparo Tomé. 2000. '"The Good Citizen": Cultural Understandings of Citizenship and Gender Amongst a New Generation of Teachers'. In *Politics, Education, and Citizenship*, edited by Mal Leicester, Celia Modgil, and Sohan Modgil, 343–67. Education, Culture, and Values, Vol. 6. London; New York: Falmer Press.

Bakunin, Mikhail. 1964. 'Power and Authority'. In *The Political Philosophy of Bakunin*, edited by G. P. Maximoff, 248–55. London; New York: The Freee Press of Glencoe.

Blau, Peter M. 1963. 'Critical Remarks on Weber's Theory of Authority'. *American Political Science Review* 57 (02): 305–16. https://doi.org/10.2307/1952824

Callan, Eamonn. 2010. *Creating Citizens: Political Education and Liberal Democracy*. Oxford Political Theory. Oxford: Clarendon Press.

De George, Richard T. 1978. 'Anarchism and Authority'. In *Anarchism*, edited by J. Roland Pennock and John W. Chapman, 91–110. Nomos, XIX. New York: New York University Press.

Advisory Group on Citizenship, 'Education for Citizenship and the Teaching of Democracy in Schools' or The Crick Report. 1998. Qualifications and Curriculum Authority.

Freidman, Milton. 1955. 'The Role of Government in Education'. In *Economics and the Public Interest*, edited by Robert A. Solo and Eugene Ewald Agger, 123–44. New Brunswick, NJ: Rutgers University Press.

Friedrich, Carl J. 1958. 'Authority, Reason, and Discretion'. In *Authority*, edited by Carl J. Friedrich, 28–48. Nomos, I. Cambridge, MA: Harvard University Press.

Galston, William A. 1991. *Liberal Purposes: Goods, Virtues, and Diversity in the Liberal State*. Cambridge Studies in Philosophy and Public Policy. Cambridge; New York: Cambridge University Press.

Gilles, Stephen G. 1996. 'On Educating Children: A Parentalist Manifesto'. *University of Chicago Law Review*, 63 (3): 937–1034.

Gintis, Herbert. 1972. 'Towards a Political Economy of Education: A Radical Critique of Ivan Illich's *Deschooling Society*'. *Harvard Educational Review* 42 (1): 70–96.

Gutmann, Amy. 1999. *Democratic Education*. Princeton, NJ; Chichester: Princeton University Press.

Hendel, Charles W. 1958. 'An Exploration of the Nature of Authority'. In *Authority*, edited by Carl J. Friedrich, 3–27. Nomos, I. Cambridge, MA: Harvard University Press.

Hershovitz, Scott. 2011. 'The Role of Authority'. *Philosophers' Imprint* 11 (7): 1–19.

Illich, Ivan. 2000. *Deschooling Society*. London: Marion Boyars.

Kropotkin, Petr Alekseevich. 1995. *The Conquest of Bread and Other Writings*. Edited by Marshall Shatz. Cambridge Texts in the History of Political Thought. Cambridge; New York: Cambridge University Press.

Levinson, Meira. 2014. *No Citizen Left Behind.* Cambridge, MA; London: Harvard University Press.

Malatesta, Errico. 2015. *Life and Ideas: The Anarchist Writings of Errico Malatesta.* Edited by Vernon Richards. Oakland: PM Press.

Marshall, Peter H. 1993. *Demanding the Impossible: A History of Anarchism.* London: Fontana Press.

McConnell, Michael W. 2002. 'Education Disestablishment: Why Democratic Values Are Ill-Served by Democratic Control of Schooling'. In *Moral and Political Education,* edited by Stephen Macedo and Yael Tamir, 87–146. Nomos, XLIII. New York: New York University Press.

McLaughlin, Terence H. 2000. 'Citizenship Education in England: The Crick Report and Beyond'. *Journal of the Philosophy of Education* 34 (4): 541–70.

Miller, David. 1984. *Anarchism.* Modern Ideologies. London: J.M. Dent.

Olssen, Mark. 2004. 'From the Crick Report to the Parekh Report: Multiculturalism, Cultural Difference, and Democracy—The Re-Visioning of Citizenship Education'. *British Journal of Sociology of Education* 25 (2): 179–92.

Osler, Audrey, and Hugh Starkey. 2001. 'Citizenship Education and National Identities in France and England: Inclusive or Exclusive?' *Oxford Review of Education* 27 (2): 287–305. https://doi.org/10.1080/03054980124800

Parekh, Bhikhu C. 2006. *Rethinking Multiculturalism: Cultural Diversity and Political Theory.* 2nd ed. Basingstoke; New York: Palgrave Macmillan.

Phillips, Anne. 2000. 'Second Class Citizenship'. In *Tomorrow's Citizens: Critical Debates in Citizenship and Education,* edited by Nick Pearce, Joe Hallgarten, and Institute for Public Policy Research, 36–42. London: IPPR.

Raz, Joseph, ed. 1990a. *Authority. Readings in Social and Political Theory.* Oxford: Basil Blackwell.

Raz, Joseph. 1990b. 'Authority and Justification'. In *Authority,* edited by Joseph Raz, 115–41. Readings in Social and Political Theory. Oxford: Basil Blackwell.

Raz, Joseph. 2006. 'The Problem of Authority: Revisiting the Service Conception'. *Minnosata Law Review* 90 (4): 1003–44.

Raz, Joseph. 2009a. *Between Authority and Interpretation: On the Theory of Law and Practical Reason.* Oxford; New York: Oxford University Press.

Raz, Joseph. 2009b. *The Morality of Freedom.* Reprinted. Oxford: Clarendon Press.

Reimer, Everett W. 1971. *School Is Dead: An Essay on Alternatives in Education.* Penguin Education Specials. Harmondsworth: Penguin.

Rosenblum, Nancy L. 1988. 'Review: Democratic Education, by Amy Gutmann'. *American Political Science Review* 82 (4): 1355–56. https://doi.org/10.2307/1961770

Sardoc, Mitja. 2018. '*Democratic Education* at 30: An Interview with Dr. Amy Gutmann'. *Theory and Research in Education* 16 (2): 244–52. https://doi.org/10.1177/1477878 518774087

Suissa, Judith. 2011. *Anarchism and Education: A Philosophical Perspective.* Oakland: PM Press.

Weber, Max. 1978. *Economy and Society: An Outline of Interpretive Sociology.* Edited by Guenther Roth and Claus Wittich. Berkeley: University of California Press.

Wolff, Robert Paul. 1998. *In Defense of Anarchism.* Berkeley: University of California Press.

Woodcock, George. 1963. *Anarchism: A HIstory of Libertarian Ideas and Movements.* Harmondsworth, Middlesex; Ringwood: Penguin Books.

Chapter 5

The interactional structure of education

Introduction

This chapter addresses the question of how the problem of authority is understood in the interactional environment. It represents the second prong that must be addressed to provide a complete answer to the tension between the individual and society. In Chapter 4, we addressed the same question but at the institutional level. Now we turn our heads to authority as it manifests in our day-to-day interactions and direct relationships and the approaches that people have taken to understand these authority relations and respond to them.

As noted in Chapter 4, in Arendt's view, authority, in a meaningful sense, and not in its equivocation with power, persuasion, or violence, has disappeared (Arendt 1993b, 91). The "most significant symptom" of the disappearance of authority from the modern world is that it is now challenged in child-rearing and education, "where authority in the widest sense has always been accepted as a natural necessity" (Arendt 1993b, 91). Arendt identifies progressive education as the source of the anti-authoritarian movement in education, which she describes as, "an astounding hodgepodge of sense and nonsense" (1993a, 178). Arendt raises this example to illustrate the depths of the crisis of authority. However, educators both inside and outside of the progressive education movement address the issue of authority to discover its legitimate foundations, much like Arendt and Weber have done in the political arena. In fact, as Christopher Winch notes,

> Authority is relevant to education not only through questions of teaching and learning (as part of a general discussion of the concept of authority) but also in politics because the provision of education as a public or semi-public good is not just a social but also a political matter; that is, it is regulated or organized by the state and set within a framework of law.
>
> (1998, 222)

Arendt is too quick to rule out the questioning of authority in education because of her perception of progressive education as something that seeks to

DOI: 10.4324/9781003271871-6

undermine legitimate authority relations. This chapter will follow the same structure as the preceding one. First, I shall offer a brief exposition of authority in the educational context which mirrors the discussion of authority in the political sphere discussed previously. Then, I shall look at the competing vision of the role of authority and the subject of Arendt's ire – progressivism, as well as the more radical elements of this approach. I will then look at the role that democratic education plays in seeking a coherent balance between the competing forces of authority and freedom in education and end with a discussion of the shortcomings of those models of democratic education.

Authority in the educational sphere

As is the case in political theory, educational theory has had to grapple with the concept of authority. The authority of the teacher and the authority of the teacher's knowledge are both points of friction when developing a model of ideal educational theory. We have seen this tension manifest in the political and educational philosophies of Rousseau, Dewey, and Freire. It was a problem that they each identified but that each, arguably, did not provide an adequate answer to. But they are not the only educators who have sought to clarify the authority relationships in the educational setting and how they are justified. R. S. Peters and Paul Nash sought to employ a Weberian analysis of authority in the classroom in order to justify the authority of the teacher and find a balance with the freedom of the child. Whereas A. S. Neill and the free school movement sought to challenge the role of authority in education and defended their view from the perspective of the child psychologist.

R. S. Peters is one of the most prominent voices in the philosophy of education. Along with Paul Hirst, Peters is credited with bringing an analytic approach of philosophy of education to the United Kingdom (Hirst and Peters 2014; Peters 2015). In *Authority, Responsibility and Education*, Peters employs Weber's tripartite analysis of authority in his discussion of its role in education (Peters 1965). Richard Pring notes, "The best general conceptual analysis of 'authority' in an educational context is to be found in Peters" (1975, 36). According to Peters, a person possesses authority when another sets aside their judgement in recognition of that authority. The teacher possesses a degree of all three types of formal authority. They possess the legal–rational authority in virtue of meeting agreed criteria; they possess the traditional authority, although this has waned over time as a result of changing public attitude; and they often possess charismatic authority, a quality that if harnessed can be used well in teaching practice but also runs the risk of abuse (Peters 1965, 16–17).

However, Peters, unlike Arendt, does not equate authority and authoritarianism (Peters 1965, 33). Arendt draws no distinction between them and argues against the "liberal" equivocation of the terms, authoritarian, totalitarian, and tyranny. According to Arendt, authoritarian government, "committed to the restriction of liberty remains tied to the freedom it limits to the extent that it would lose its very substance if it abolished it altogether" (Arendt 1993b, 96). Whereas this is not the case for a totalitarian government which aims for the total elimination of freedom and tyranny which rules in accordance with the will and interest of a single person rather than the law (Arendt 1993b, 96). But this difference between Arendt and Peters is purely terminological.

Peters argues that it is a delicate balance between coercion and authority that the teacher must tread for it is the responsibility of the teacher to cultivate the morality of existing society through their teaching, but it is also the responsibility of the teacher to cultivate pupils' ability to correct perceived mistakes. Peters writes, "a teacher must both be an authority and teach in such a way that pupils become capable of showing him where he is wrong. The teacher is an agent of change and challenge as well as of cultural conservation" (1966, 9). There is the authority that comes with social control and the authority that comes with one's expertise. Richard Pring notes that "The distinction here is that between 'in authority' and being 'an authority'" (1975, 24).

In his discussion of authority, Peters draws apart the notions of teaching, instruction, and indoctrination. Indoctrination, of which there is no legitimate expression, "involves either merely the inculcation of beliefs or the addition of a rationale which discourages the evaluation of beliefs—e.g. the appeal to authority as a backing" (Peters 1966, 9). Instruction is similar to indoctrination but encourages, "the probing of principles at a later stage", when the child is at the right stage of development, and is therefore, according to Peters, sometimes necessary, especially with younger children (Peters 1966, 9). Teaching is neither of these things, instead it, "involves the passing on of knowledge, skills, or modes of conduct in such a way that the learner is brought to understand and evaluate the underlying rationale for what is presented to him" (Peters 1966, 9). What this means, for Peters, is that while the teacher is an authority, in many ways, they are more than merely an authority. It is a part of the skill of a teacher to know when to express their authority as a command to be followed without evaluation of beliefs on the part of the subject. If a teacher falls into unnecessary instruction, or does so in an authoritarian or doctrinaire manner, they risk arresting a child's ability to move from reliance upon authority to developing their own reliable judgement. Charismatic authority enhances this danger because it is unreliable and unstable, dependent as it is on the individual who wields that authority and their relationship with those that recognise it. Therefore, in Peters' formulation of authority in the classroom, the teacher possesses authority, it is a property of the teacher, but they must express authority with caution over the children for fear of straying into authoritarian teaching. However, in Peters' view, as Winch notes, authority is not necessary in society outside of schools. Only those situations, such as in the school environment where children have not developed their full psychological self, "require the participation of an authority" (Winch 1998, 222).

Paul Nash expresses a similar conception of authority as Peters. Nash accepts the concept of authority as a property of the teacher and seeks to find the balance of expression on behalf of the teacher. Nash recognises a distinction between authority and authoritarianism and condemns the latter while recognising the necessity of the former, in much the same way as Peters. He writes,

> The necessity for avoiding the personality degeneration associated with authoritarianism does not absolve the teacher from the responsibilities of leadership. It only makes the task of leading more subtle and difficult. To abdicate leadership is no better—and may be worse—than to wield authoritarian control.
>
> (1966, 104)

It is safe to understand Nash's use of the word "leadership", as equivalent to Arendt's use of "rule". However, it is important to note that a teacher's rule is distinct from a government's rule according to Arendt. She writes, "If rule is at all involved here, it is entirely different from political forms of rule, not only because it is limited in time and intent, but because it happens between people who are potentially equals" (1993b, 118).

It has been claimed that Geoffrey Herman Bantock shares a similar understanding of authority to Peters as well (Kitchen 2014), but this is unfair to Peters. In fact, Bantock defends a very two-dimensional conception of authority where he equates authority with power and authoritarianism. After claiming that, "The school necessarily involves an authoritative set-up", Bantock seamlessly moves from discussion of authority to write, "Power is an inescapable element in adult life, to which we all at some time or other have to come to terms" (1970, 188).

We can interpret Peters and Nash as walking the line between extremes. They argue that the imposition of authority is sometimes necessary in the school and in the classroom and warn against the dangers of too much or too little authority. They attempt to illustrate a way in which we can retain authority while not imposing upon the freedom of others. In contrast, there are, of course, calls for greater authority and discipline in school as well as calls for greater freedom. While appeals for a strong hand in school are heard regularly in populist political rhetoric, few contemporary writers interested in educational theory and practice advocate authoritarian control by teachers. Although they can be found if one looks hard enough. Diane Ravitch and Eric D. Hirsch are the most often-cited defenders of traditional or didactic education in schools (Ravitch 1985; Hirsch 1999, 2016), but even of these boogie monsters of progressive education, it is unfair to suggest that they promote a strict authoritarianism.

Another person who can be seen to support a more authoritarian approach to education is Mary Haywood Metz. Metz defends a rights-based definition of authority and drew upon the work of Weber and Durkheim in the formulation of her conception of authority. She writes,

> Authority is the right of a person in a specified role to give commands to which a person in another specified role has a duty to render obedience. This rights and duty rest upon the superordinate's recognised status as the legitimate representative of a moral order to which both superordinate and subordinate owe allegiance.
>
> (1978, 27)

Within Metz's conception of authority, coercion is not clearly separated. Pace and Hemmings write of Metz's conceptualisation of authority that, "teachers may use coercion. This includes tactics such as reprimanding or embarrassing students, making them move their seats, sending them out of the classroom, giving them detention, and expelling or failing them" (2006, 8).

In contrast to these limited expressions of strong authority relations in educational settings, there exists an alternative approach to education that, amongst other things, reinterprets the role of authority in the interactions between teacher and student. This approach came to prominence in the nineteenth and twentieth centuries, but its roots are found in the philosophy of Rousseau and, in particular, his pedagogical novel *Émile*.

The alternative and the radical

Progressivism is a broad term and defined variously. However, John Darling and Erik Nordenbo highlight five themes which, "echo throughout its history" (2003, 295). These are as follows: a criticism of traditional education; a challenge to understandings of the nature of knowledge; the view that children possess a natural desire to learn; a commitment to the value of democracy in schools because of children's right to determine their own learning; and a commitment to the development of the whole person (Darling and Nordenbo 2003, 295–308). Progressivism, understood in this way, is an approach to education with which Rousseau, Dewey, and Freire are often associated.

Rousseau is a key figure in progressive education. Darling and Nordenbo write, "the first of the classics in the history of progressivism [was] Rousseau. … and perhaps the first writer to advance the idea of what we now sometimes call a child-centred approach to education" (2003, 289). Rousseau located learning in a child's interaction with the world rather than in their instruction by the teacher. Progressivism is intimately linked to this child-centred approach. Dewey too holds a prominent position within the progressive education tradition, and his influence is felt throughout the Western world. In the United Kingdom, Dewey's philosophy was instrumental in the formation of the Plowden Report published in 1967. Freire, while more commonly referred to as a member of the critical pedagogy movement, is often cited as a progressive educator also (English and Stengel 2010). Even though his theory exists within a different approach, the overlaps are clear enough that the connection is often made between progressive education and critical pedagogy (Kellner 2003, 51–64). Rousseau, Dewey, and Freire each seek to develop a child-centred or progressive model of education that seeks to overcome the tension between the individual and society through social justice in a way that it would be difficult to attribute to any other.

According to the five themes of progressive education as identified by Darling and Nordenbo, the problem of authority is not a necessary concern of the progressive educator; however, it is easy to see how the problem of authority arises as a consequence of those themes. In challenging the nature of knowledge, the traditional understanding of the teacher as the possessor and disseminator of a fixed body of knowledge is also questioned. Coupled with the commitment to the value of democracy in schools, the shift in power relations is evident. What is learnt and how it is learnt become debated but not solely by the professionals and academics. The children themselves have a voice in their own learning. Therefore, neither the teacher nor the school, in a progressive educational model, possess unquestioned authority. They, instead, appear to be in the same position as the government of a liberal democratic state and seek to find a balance between the freedom of democratic participants and the authority of their institution.

A. S. Neill became a figurehead of the progressive education movement. He established Summerhill School in 1921 and shaped the schools philosophy and educational practice on principles arrived at through child psychology. He argued that adult-imposed requirements may make a child fear that they cannot live up to the expectations of the adult. The children then become anxious about losing the love and approval of the adult. In Neill's view, this problem is made worse if the rules are presented as moral rules because it then adds the element of guilt. In addition to this, the anxiety of authority which results from the tension between a child's desires and the rules they are forced to live by produces hatred. Neill believed that a child hates to be restricted and suppressed and will hate the person responsible for this suppression. This authoritative disciplining produces self-hatred because forcing a child to be good conveys the message that what they want to do is bad, thereby teaching the child to hate their inclinations and, by extension, themselves.

Additionally, the imposition of authority limits a person's ability to make decisions for themselves. Therefore, the removal of this imposition, as Darling notes, "means that pupils learn how to handle freedom and how to take responsibility for their conduct and learning" (1992, 48). However, for Neill, the removal of authority in this manner is not the rule itself but a consequence of the primary principle of unconditional love. Unconditional love is needed to break through the expectations of children towards adults. To borrow terminology from Homer Lane, a major influence on Neill's approach to education, children needed to know that the adults were "on their side".

A wonderful example of this is given by Lane: a young child is sentenced by the magistrate to attend The Little Commonwealth reformatory for being caught stealing; Lane entrusts him to make his own way there and provides him with the train fare. Lane writes, "Tim came to the Commonwealth, not because my personality overcame him, but because my love for him released his own true personality" (1969, 176).

As such, authority, understood as the undemocratic assertion of power over another, should be removed from the child's world, leaving behind self-governing cooperative authority. David Carr summarises this thought well when he writes that, "until troubled children had been liberated from the negative associations of (parental, educational or other) authority, it would be impossible for them to recognise the intrinsic life-enhancing purpose and utility of the norms of civilised life" (2003, 226). The result of the practice of self-government is the promotion of responsible self-direction and the promotion of authentic responsibility in a climate of mutual respect and trust.

Neill advocated for the removal of adult authority, but he drew a distinction between freedom and licence. In Summerhill, Neill drew the scope of individual freedom thusly, "each individual is free to do what he likes as long as he is not trespassing on the freedom of others" (1968, 309). Neill believes that the consequence of this definition of freedom is an equal sharing of responsibilities and rights – there being no such thing as complete or absolute freedom. Absolute freedom, or freedom without qualification, is a freedom of conflict because it necessarily impinges upon the freedom of others. Therefore, freedom must be, to some degree, limited. Neill writes, "There isn't such a thing as absolute freedom. Anyone who allows a child to get all his own way is following a dangerous path" (1968, 309).

The legitimate expression of authority is this limitation which imposes certain constraints upon people in the name of freedom. The line between freedom and authority that Neill draws is between the private and the public sphere. This is what Neill would call the difference between individual freedom and social freedom. An action that affects the interests only of the actor cannot be limited. In the case of Summerhill, an example is going to class. Whereas throwing stones is another matter. There are justifiable rules governing social life. Authority, therefore, does still exist, but it is not of one (or a few) over others but the authority of the community over each other.

Discipline and licence occur when the balance between freedom and authority has not been found. Discipline and licence have an inverse relation where all the rights are held by either the subject or the object. For the unfree child, there are two possible circumstances: either the teachers have all the rights and children have no rights, or the children have all the rights and the teachers have no rights. The former example is what Neill calls discipline and the latter licence (Neill 1968, 267–69). Neither instance contributes towards freedom. Freedom is the practice of equal rights for both parties. Neil writes, "in the disciplined home, the children have no rights. In the spoiled home, they have all the rights. The proper home is one in which children and adults have equal rights. And the same applies to school" (1968, 105). This is consistent with the types of freedom defended by Rousseau, Dewey, and Freire because it is a freedom of constraints which are self-imposed and represent means to further freedom.

It is unclear, however, if Neill's pedagogical model finds a coherent balance between freedom and authority. Neill has been widely criticised for permitting too much freedom and compromising the education of his students as a result (Gutmann 1999, 89; Carr 2003, 227). Or, equally troubling, it is unclear whether Summerhill presents an educational model that is scalable beyond the limited scope of a small independent boarding school. After all, Neill's Summerhill represents but one half of the progressive education movement in the United Kingdom. Inspired by educators such as Neill, the 1960s and 1970s saw an attempt to bring the principles of Summerhill and make them accessible to all. This is often characterised as the free school movement. Few of these schools stayed open for long. Wright estimates that, out of all attempts made to open free schools, only fourteen or fifteen of them can be said to have succeeded in becoming properly established (1989). None of them remain open today. White Lion Street School, one of the most successful free schools, closed its doors in 1990. I shall return to a consideration of the practices of White Lion Street School in Chapter 7 as I aim to defend the internally democratic schooling from its detractors.

The interactional response of democratic education

In Chapter 4, we looked at the role of democratic education in reference to the institutional structure of education. The purpose of this section is to look at contemporary practice in the educational environment that shapes the interactional structure of education and how that relates to the tension between the individual and society and, more specifically, to the problem of authority.

It is clear that, for the most part and for the vast majority of learners, school remains an authoritarian environment. We may not suffer the vocal or physical discipline of the stereotypical Victorian teacher exemplified by Mr. Gradgrind of Dickins' novel *Hard Times*, but it takes little observation and only a short conversation with a student to understand that a significant amount of energy in school is spent on behaviour management. Teachers employ a host of techniques and methods in order to maintain control of their students and, in turn, their classroom. This is justified in a number of ways, and it is often understandable why a teacher exerts such strict control – class sizes are large, unruly students are common, children have short attention spans and a tendency to distract one another, there are often students who require greater attention than others, school days are long, and teacher demands are high. Strict control is seen as the most effective method of progressing students from one learning objective to another.

There are spaces where this expression of authority for the purposes of behaviour management is lessened and the students are encouraged to question and engage in a way distinct from their everyday learning, but these spaces are not universal, and many students will complete their compulsory education with no taste of a different interactional environment. Most limiting is that these opportunities are very dependent on the professional commitment of individual teachers and third-party organisations. For the purposes of the arguments made here, the most important of these alternative interactional spaces to discuss is that created by citizenship education and third-party education specialists who aim to cultivate the development of the person – there are numerous examples but I shall isolate UNICEF's Rights Respecting Schools Award (RRSA), the aim of which is to empower students using the UN Convention on the Rights of the Child (CRC) as the backbone of learning and discovery.

I discussed aspects of *The Crick Report* in Chapter 4, as part of the institutional structure of education within the United Kingdom. However, it is worth returning to here in virtue of citizenship education being a compulsory subject from the age of thirteen (Year 9/KS3) and because of the role that *The Crick Report* played in informing the pedagogical principles as well as the content of citizenship education in England and Wales since its publication in 1998.

While Crick refers to the view expressed by the report as one of civic republicanism, it takes on distinctly liberal notions also (Crick 1999; 2004; 2011). It places itself within the narrative of the classical debate and as such follows on from the liberal theory of T. H. Marshall and of Bernard Weatherill's Commission on Citizenship, *Encouraging Citizenship: Report of the Commission on Citizenship* (1990), hereafter referred to as *The Weatherill Report*. In the case of the former, *The Crick Report* retains the three elements of citizenship identified by Marshall in 'Citizenship and Social Class': the civil, the political, and the social (Marshall 1950). The civil element stresses a reciprocity between rights and duties; the social adds to the welfare state defended by Marshall a focus on community and voluntary engagement; and the political element emphasises the importance of political understanding and action which will inform one's civic spirit and voluntary activity (*The Crick Report* 1998, 9–13). This is done with the aim of developing a form of "active citizenship".

The Crick Report adds the stronger tones of "active citizenship" from *The Weatherill Report* to Marshall's three elements of a citizen but supposedly goes beyond both because neither Marshall nor *The Weatherill Report* focus on the importance of learning political understanding and action. *The Crick Report* states,

> Perhaps it took political citizenship for granted (which, historically, it has never been safe to do). Civic spirit, citizens' charters and voluntary activity in the community are of crucial importance, but individuals must be

helped and prepared to shape the terms of such engagements by political understanding and action.

(The Crick Report 1998, 10)

With this in mind, one can describe the citizen of The Crick Report as a person with rights and responsibilities across the three elements of the citizen. The citizen of The Crick Report embodies, in the plainest terms, the tension between the individual and society that persists in all conceptions of the citizen. Additionally, The Crick Report includes within its conception of the citizen a respect for the rule of law (The Crick Report 1998, 10). The strength of this proclamation is mitigated somewhat by an encouragement to see the difference between law and justice. The report states, "Citizens must be equipped with the political skills needed to change laws in a peaceful and responsible manner" (The Crick Report 1998, 10). Therefore, the citizens of The Crick Report must find the balance between their being subject to the laws of the society of which they are a part, and an active challenger of those laws. This feature of the citizen emphasises both the rights of the individual as well as the individual's responsibility to the state and their local, national, and global communities. Furthermore, these rights and responsibilities are not solely to be enjoyed passively. The citizen of The Crick Report is an active member of society through voluntary and political action and awareness.

The aims of citizenship education in The Crick Report are identified by the declared learning outcomes. The learning outcomes recommended by The Crick Report are separated into four categories: concepts; values and dispositions; skills and aptitudes; and knowledge and understanding. A complete statement or overview of what is required in citizenship education by the end of compulsory schooling is covered by these four categories. This is a particular approach to curricula which focusses primarily on achieving clearly established goals. This is in contrast to content-based models which construct curricula upon and organise them around a largely unquestioned fixed set of knowledge and process models which shift the focus of curricula away from the content learnt and turn instead to the pedagogical practices which are employed to cultivate learning (McCowan 2009, 92).

Therefore, the interactional environment for learning envisaged by The Crick Report cannot assume a traditional relationship between teacher and student. While there are elements of transferring knowledge within citizenship education so imagined, they are restricted primarily to the learning of the existing institutional structure and mode of government. Outside of this, The Crick Report aims to cultivate values through engagement and encourage young people to challenge the existing state of affairs within certain parameters. This cannot be done within an environment of instruction and correct or fixed answers. There must be a certain degree of dialogue and discussion; there must be some give and take between the students and the teachers. Therefore, the authority of the teacher cannot overwhelm the autonomy of the students – it cannot be absolute, but by the same token, the questioning and dialogue is designed to take place within quite a limited scope exemplified by the recent move to prohibit external groups from teaching in schools if their teaching or aims undermine the fundamental British values by promoting what are understood as extreme political positions. Extreme political positions include the promotion of non-democratic ideology and the violent overthrow of capitalism ("Political Impartiality in Schools" 2022). On first glance, this may seem unproblematic, but it is a clear manifestation of the principle of self-preservation writ large and a deeply embedded hypocrisy. There are many instances of undemocratic and anti-democratic activity within existing British "democracy", such as the existence of the House of Lords, the practice of the first-past-the-post electoral system, the competing influences on the actions of the representatives of democracy (party, ideology, government, constituents, the interests of the nation or local community, etc.), the presence of the monarchy, and the non-existent powers of the public in holding their representatives to account and demanding an opportunity to exercise their democratic power through elections. Coupled with the fact that the state claims an exclusive right to the use of violent force, whether that be through the police service or the armed forces, it seems clear that any prohibition on the teachings of force and undemocratic behaviour is disingenuous. It is unlikely that the state wishes to legislate against their own activity. In fact, their own undemocratic institutions and practices and their use of force are protected under the title of "democracy" and become difficult to challenge for fear of transgressing the prohibition against teaching an "extreme political position". We can therefore only conclude that the intention, whether consciously or otherwise, is to prohibit teaching that could undermine a state like this.

In addition to mandatory citizenship education, there are numerous education initiatives in the United Kingdom which aim to offer an alternative model of citizenship or character education. For example, there are Cooperative Schools, Forest Schools, Human Scale Education, Learn to Lead, Learning without Limits, and RSA Opening Minds that each offer a tailored response to the increasing demand on our pupils to achieve high test scores in didactic learning environments. One such initiative which I shall look at in more detail is the RRSA, which is developed by UNICEF and practised within the United Kingdom to some level by nearly 5,000 schools. The RRSA started in 2004 and helps schools to use the United Nations Convention of the Rights of the Child (CRC) as their values framework. There are four key areas of impact for children at a Rights Respecting School: wellbeing, participation, relationships, and self-esteem. These four areas are reached through three strands: teaching and learning about rights; teaching and learning through rights – ethos and relationships; and teaching and learning for rights – participation, empowerment, and action.

In the first strand the children learn what their rights are as persons with reference to the CRC, and teachers, non-teaching staff, and carers are also made to learn the CRC. Together, "this shared understanding [is used] to work for improved child wellbeing, school improvement, global justice and sustainable living" ("The Rights Respecting Schools Award Strands – UNICEF UK"). The second strand represents the practice of employing one's rights inside the school and in accordance with the values attached to the rights of the CRC. To quote from the UNICEF website,

> Children, young people and adults collaborate to develop and maintain a school community based on equality, dignity, respect, nondiscrimination and participation; this includes learning and teaching in a way that respects the rights of both educators and learners and promotes wellbeing.
> ("The Rights Respecting Schools Award Strands – UNICEF UK")

The third strand encompasses the passive enjoyment of rights, the active application of one's rights, and empowerment to promote the rights of others locally and globally. Evidence of teaching these three strands will result in a school being accredited by UNICEF as a Rights Respecting School.

Research on the effects within schools is quite limited, but initial findings are quite positive. The largest study on Rights Respecting Schools has been conducted by Judy Sebba and Carol Robinson, and they found that the education initiative, "had a profound effect on the majority of schools involved in the programme. For some school communities, there is strong evidence that it has been a life-changing experience" (2010, 3). The main findings relate to six indicators: knowledge and understanding of the CRC; relationships and behaviour; pupils' attitudes of empowerment towards the environment and the rights of others locally, nationally, and globally; pupil's ability to demonstrate positive attitudes towards an inclusive and diverse society; pupils' level of active participation in the decision-making of their school; and pupil attainment. Additionally, Katherine Covell explores the impact of Rights Respecting Schools in Hampshire (Covell 2010). Evidence in Hampshire of their Rights Respecting Responsibility (RRR) initiative, which is tied closely to the UNICEF RRSA, indicates an increase in pupil engagement according to both teacher and the pupils. UNICEF's more recent impact report, "Creating Active and Engaged Citizens" (2018), supports these findings as does other research into RRSA. As Ally Dunhill notes, the RRSA, "confirms that teaching and supporting the human rights of children to children, through a rights education programme, encourages children to practice, protect and promote the rights of others within their school" (2018, 24).

The Crick Report and the RRSA have laudable aims and should be celebrated for expanding the scope of the school beyond the accumulation of facts in a limited number of subjects but it is unclear if they are able to successfully address the problem of authority or the larger tension between the individual and society. A defender of these projects could easily side-step my concern by stating that it is not in the purview of these projects to address these issues. What they do is seek to empower students with more than knowledge, and they seek to encourage an emotional and cultural attachment to their social environment, to cultivate a sense of justice beyond their own private interests, and a passion for political engagement. However, in virtue of the subject matter they discuss and the aims that they hold, projects of this kind wade deep into the waters of the problem of authority *because* they seek to empower young people. In doing so, they challenge our traditional ideas of authority and the role of the child, but if these programmes are designed with this aim in mind, they remain largely silent on it. As such, it is unclear that either of the projects that I have used as examples of democratic education in the interactional sphere adequately address this problem the authority, instead turning it into an insidious force that compels and coerces in the undercurrents of the psychology of the child – reminiscent of the Tutor's treatment of Émile.

In opposition to democratic education

There has been a shift in policy since the implementation of compulsory citizenship education in England and Wales and this shift is illustrative of a political and ideological shift away from the political literacy of Bernard Crick and towards a more communitarian volunteerism promoted by some members of the British Conservative Party. Since its inception in 2002, there has been substantive change in the curriculum which has led citizenship education away from the original sentiments of *The Crick Report*. There has been a definite move away from the outcome model of curriculum and towards a content model. The most recent iteration of the curriculum was introduced in 2014 and focusses primarily on the knowledge that each person should gain and not the skills, concepts, and values that were also central to the curriculum previously. Lee Jerome identifies the change in the role that rights and responsibilities play within the curriculum as a key indicator of the move. He writes,

> In 2007 the curriculum included a range of content and guidance to explain how rights developed in different contexts, often through a process of struggle, and that responsibilities varied between individual, communities and government and thus opened up the concept to critical exploration. By contrast, the 2014 curriculum limits itself to the observation that, in relation to the underlying concepts, the curriculum should "develop" ... and then "deepen" "pupils' understanding of... the rights and responsibilities of citizens".
>
> (2018, 487)

Jerome identifies, in addition to the Department for Education's stated aim to focus on essential knowledge, an ideological bias present in the language of the new curriculum. Jerome highlights the phrase "precious liberties enjoyed" as illustrative of this bias in that instead of pupils learning the struggle for rights, as they did previously, they now are to be taught of passively enjoyed freedoms which "should be appreciated as 'precious', which implies a somewhat reverential tone" (2018, 487).

Furthermore, a change has occurred in the aims of citizenship education alongside the United Kingdom's governmental response to terrorism. The Prevent Strategy presented to Parliament by the Secretary of State for the Home Department in June 2011 outlined, amongst other things, the government's plans to minimise the risk of children and vulnerable people being "radicalised" (*Prevent Strategy* 2011). The Prevent Strategy defines radicalisation as "the process by which a person comes to support terrorism and forms of extremism leading to terrorism" (2011, 108). Terrorism is defined by UK law in the Terrorism Act 2000 Section 1, as a violent act performed in order to influence the government and advance some political, religious, or ideological causes (*Terrorism Act* 2000). Therefore, I see little controversy in a governmental strategy to minimise the risk of terrorist acts. However, the Prevent Strategy defines extremism as, "vocal or active opposition to fundamental British values, including democracy, the rule of law, individual liberty and mutual respect and tolerance of different faiths and beliefs" (2011, 107). This definition has been a cause of some concern.

The recently published report by the Select Committee on Citizenship and Civic Engagement titled *The Ties That Bind* recommended that fundamental British values be reframed as "Shared Values of British Citizenship" because "It should recognise that the values are both shared with people from other countries and are essentially British" (*The Ties That Bind* 2018, 18). However, in addition to this, it is important to take note that democracy as a form of rule and the rule of law are both defined as essential values of the British citizen. Therefore, the existing authority relations are defined as necessary in society and in the individual.

Accompanying the changes in citizenship education, it was noted in *The Ties That Bind* that there has been a decline in citizenship education within the United Kingdom. The decline in citizenship education has a number of contributing factors according to the report. One of which is the revision of the national curriculum in 2014. The other reasons cited are the academisation of schools, meaning a reduction in schools where it is compulsory to teach citizenship education; that the subject appears to be held in relatively low esteem; and that there has been a marked decrease in the numbers of teachers training as Citizenship Education specialists which accompanies a decrease in the numbers of students who sit the Citizenship GCSE (*The Ties That Bind* 2018, 4–5).

A further concern raised by *The Ties That Bind* is with respect to the United Kingdom's approach to what constitutes an "active citizen". The meaning of which has shifted with the political landscape since the publication of *The Crick Report*. No longer is the active citizen a politically engaged person but primarily one who is engaged within their local and national communities through their voluntary associations. In the report it is written, "Active citizenship is too often defined purely in terms of volunteering, social action, or learning facts, and too rarely in terms of learning about and practicing democracy in the sense of political engagement and democratic participation" (*The Ties That Bind* 2018, 10). This charge is levelled at both compulsory and post-compulsory citizenship programmes.

A major source of this shift is found in the influence of "modernisers" within the British Conservative Party. When the popularity of the Conservative Party waned under the burden of Thatcherism in the 1990s, political alternatives gained popularity within the party. One such thread was communitarianism (Willetts 1994). With the launch of David Cameron's Big Society in 2010, this communitarian ideology became the mainstream conservative platform.[1] Cameron's Big Society aimed at developing policies which encouraged community action and dissolved certain powers into these communities. This has been described as a move away from the strong individualism and libertarian influence of Thatcherism that was dominant throughout the 1980s, but there are themes which persist (Ellison 2011; Wiggan 2011). This is because both seek to decentralise authority and place the burden of responsibility upon the individuals, whether that be in the context of their community or not. The National Citizenship Service (NCS) announced by the then Prime Minister David Cameron in 2010, and formally established through the *National Citizen Service Act* (2017), was a flagship government programme which reflected these communitarian sympathies.

The conservative communitarianism that has been assurgent over the last twenty years has shifted the conception of the citizen away from Crick's emphasis on the political. Reflected in the subsequent iterations of the curriculum for citizenship education, the concept of active citizenship has returned to something more reminiscent of *The Weatherill Report* (1990). The civic spirit of Weatherill's active citizen trades little on political understanding and action, focussing instead on citizen's charters and voluntary action in their community. They are, in the typology of Joel Westheimer and Joseph Kahne, examples of the responsible citizen, who is actively engaged and responsible towards themselves and their community; and the participatory citizen, "who actively participate[s] in the civic affairs and the social life of the community at the local, state, or national level" (Westheimer and Kahne 2004, 241). What they are not is an example of the social-justice-oriented citizen, who possesses the skills to "analyse and understand the interplay of social, economic, and political forces" (Westheimer and Kahne 2004, 242).

The Crickean citizen has morphed over time into something new as a result of this communitarian trend; however, the communitarian critique is not the only source of challenge to Crick's model of citizenship education. As noted in Chapter 4, even in its original framing before the introduction of fundamental British values, there was a concern that the Crickean citizen did not sufficiently consider the interests and values of those in the margins of society. This is both an institutional and interactional reality of *The Crick Report*. It is supported institutionally by the content of the curriculum and the political structure that seeks to retain its power to govern; and it is supported interactionally by the realisation of these prejudices in classroom practice, through the operation of the white-dominant culture as both the positive realisation of the citizen and the neutral standard by which alternatives are understood.

Rights Respecting Schools have not received the critical attention that *The Crick Report* has, not least because it is a small project by comparison and is not a part of compulsory education, but it is not without drawbacks. In drawing young people's attention to the rights of young people, the RRSA creates a fascinating tension in the relationship between teacher and student. For example, they will learn that they have the right to an education but because they are not given the tools or authority to enforce that right, the education given becomes dangerously disingenuous and empty of value. The young people may have the right to an education and have that right protected in law, but what form that education takes is kept from them. Are they to receive an education directed by the interests of present society for the jobs that are most needed? Are they to receive an education directed by the values and knowledge of the adults of the present generation and have that imposed upon them? Or, should this right to an education extend to include the power to shape that education by the young people themselves. In other words, should it be directed by economic interests, political interest, or individual interest?

Intimately related to this is the question of how this knowledge of rights and power (or lack of) ought to shape the relationship between the young people and their teachers. Again, just like in citizenship education shaped by *The Crick Report*, the traditional mould of the teacher as instructor of knowledge and holder of authority is not suitable for an interactional environment where young people are to be empowered. There must be dialogue, discussion, and challenge. The question is whether this is possible within the limited scope and control exemplified by drawing the lines around a non-binding convention written and signed by the state such as the CRC.

Conclusion

In the final two chapters of this book, I present detailed accounts of the interactional and institutional structures of education that seem best placed to resolve the tension between the individual and society and realise the Critical Citizen. This constitutes two answers, one primarily addressing the interactional concerns and the other primarily addressing the institutional concerns. Two answers that are designed to be pursued concurrently. In Chapter 6, I shall argue that the institutional structure of education best suited for the realisation of the Critical Citizen is one that incorporates the democratic voice of all interested parties in the educational lives of its members, but that no one's voice should be greater than the educand. This aim is achieved by removing the vested interest of existing power relations beyond the protection of basic rights and emphasising the participation of the local community in the school and the school in the local community. This model I shall refer to as the federated disestablishment of education and state.

In the final chapter, I shall argue that the interactional structure of education that is best suited for the realisation of the Critical Citizen is one of internally democratic schooling which employs a Freirean problem-posing pedagogy (Freire 2017). I argue that internally democratic problem-posing education mitigates the coercive aspects of one's social environment by creating a schooling environment which enfranchises the pupils and encourages the development of the person through dialogue with one's peers. Furthermore, I argue that through the practice of a problem-posing model of education within the framework of internally democratic schools' pupils are best placed to develop the skills needed to meaningfully participate in society once they leave school because they have developed those skills through experiment and practise within their school environment. Furthermore, in this space and through this pedagogical method, values and beliefs are established by participatory pupils in conversation with the world rather than in competition with the world. The picture that I paint is one of a federated disestablishment of education and state, and alongside internally democratic schooling, a new and radical political and educational framework is presented.

Note

1 Although, as an aside, the recent instability within the British Conservative Party means that it is difficult to accurately assess the ascendant ideology among its members and parliamentarians.

References

Arendt, Hannah. 1993a. 'The Crisis in Education'. In *Between Past and Future: Eight Exercises in Political Thought*, 173–96. New York: Penguin Books.
Arendt, Hannah. 1993b. 'What Is Authority?' In *Between Past and Future: Eight Exercises in Political Thought*, 91–141. New York: Penguin Books.
Bantock, Geoffrey Herman. 1970. *Freedom and Authority in Education: A Criticism of Modern Cultural and Educational Assumptions*. London: Faber and Faber.

Carr, David. 2003. *Making Sense of Education: An Introduction to the Philosophy and Theory of Education and Teaching*. London and New York: Routledge Falmer.

Covell, Katherine. 2010. 'School Engagement and Rights-Respecting Schools'. *Cambridge Journal of Education* 40 (1): 39–51.

'Creating Active and Engaged Citizens'. 2018. UNICEF.

Crick, Bernard. 1999. 'The Presuppositions of Citizenship Education'. *Journal of Philosophy of Education* 33 (3): 337–52. https://doi.org/10.1111/1467-9752.00141

Crick, Bernard. 2004. *Essays on Citizenship*. Continuum Studies in Citizenship. London and New York: Continuum.

Crick, Bernard. 2011. *In Defence of Politics*. London: Bloomsbury Publishing.

Darling, John. 1992. 'A. S. Neill on Democratic Authority: A Lesson from Summerhill?' *Oxford Review of Education* 18 (1): 45–57. https://doi.org/10.1080/030549 8920180104

Darling, John, and Erik Nordenbo. 2003. 'Progressivism'. In *The Blackwell Guide to the Philosophy of Education*, edited by Nigel Blake, Paul Smeyers, Richard D. Smith, and Paul Standish, 288–308. Oxford: Blackwell Publishing.

Dunhill, Ally. 2018. 'Does Teaching Children about Human Rights, Encourage Them to Practice, Protect and Promote the Rights of Others?' *Education 3–13* 46 (1): 16–26. https://doi.org/10.1080/03004279.2016.1165717

Advisory Group on Citizenship, 'Education for Citizenship and the Teaching of Democracy in Schools' or The Crick Report. 1998. Qualifications and Curriculum Authority.

Ellison, Nick. 2011. 'The Conservative Party and the Big Society'. In *Social Policy Review 23: Analysis and Debate in Social Policy, 2011*, edited by Chris Holden, Majella Kilkey, and Gaby Ramia, 45–62. Bristol: Policy Press. http://public.eblib. com/choice/publicfullrecord.aspx?p=744797

English, Andrea, and Barbara Stengel. 2010. 'Exploring Fear: Rousseau, Dewey, and Freire on Fear and Learning'. *Educational Theory* 60 (5): 521–42. https://doi. org/10.1111/j.1741-5446.2010.00375.x

Freire, Paulo. 2017. *Pedagogy of the Oppressed*. Translated by Myra Bergman Ramos. London, England: Penguin Books.

Gutmann, Amy. 1999. *Democratic Education*. Princeton, NJ and Chichester: Princeton University Press.

Hirsch, E. D. 1999. *The Schools We Need and Why We Don't Have Them*. Anchor Books. New York: Doubleday.

Hirsch, E. D. 2016. *Why Knowledge Matters: Rescuing Our Children from Failed Educational Theories*. Cambridge, MA: Harvard Education Press.

Hirst, Paul Heywood, and R. S. Peters. 2014. *The Logic of Education*. London and New York: Routledge.

Secretary of State for the Home Department. 2011. *Prevent Strategy*. London: H. M. Stationery Office.

Jerome, Lee. 2018. 'What Do Citizens Need to Know? An Analysis of Knowledge in Citizenship Curricula in the UK and Ireland'. *Compare: A Journal of Comparative and International Education* 48 (4): 483–99.

Kellner, Douglas. 2003. 'Toward a Critical Theory of Education'. *Democracy & Nature* 9 (1): 51–64.

Kitchen, William H. 2014. *Authority and the Teacher*. London: Bloomsbury Academic, an imprint of Bloomsbury Publishing.

Lane, Homer. 1969. *Talks to Parents and Teachers*. New York: Schocken Books.

Marshall, T. H. 1950. 'Citizenship and Social Class'. In *Citizenship and Social Class and Other Essays*, 1–85. London and New York: Cambridge University Press.

McCowan, Tristan. 2009. *Rethinking Citizenship Education: A Curriculum for Participatory Democracy*. Continuum Studies in Educational Research. London and New York: Continuum.

Metz, Mary Haywood. 1978. *Classrooms and Corridors: The Crisis of Authority in Desegregated Secondary Schools*. Berkeley: University of California Press.

Nash, Paul. 1966. *Authority and Freedom in Education: An Introduction to the Philosophy of Education*. New York; London; Sydney: John Wiley & Sons Inc.

National Citizen Service Act. 2017.

Neill, Alexander Sutherland. 1968. *Summerhill*. Pelican Books. Harmondsworth: Penguin Books.

Pace, Judith L., and Annette B. Hemmings. 2006. 'Understanding Classroom Authority as a Social Construction'. In *Classroom Authority: Theory, Research, and Practice*, edited by Judith L. Pace and Annette B. Hemmings, 1–32. Mahwah, NJ: L. Erlbaum Associates.

Peters, R. S. 1965. *Authority, Responsibility and Education*. 2nd ed. Northampton: George Allen and Unwin.

Peters, R. S. 1966. 'The Authority of the Teacher'. *Comparative Education* 3 (1): 1–12.

Peters, R. S. 2015. *Ethics and Education*. Oxford and New York: George Allen and Unwin.

'Political Impartiality in Schools'. 2022. GOV.UK. 17 February 2022. https://www.gov.uk/government/publications/political-impartiality-in-schools/political-impartiality-in-schools

Pring, Richard. 1975. 'In Defence of Authority - or How to Keep Knowledge under Control'. In *Values and Authority in Schools*, edited by David Bridges and Peter Scrimshaw, 20–37. London: Hodder and Stoughton.

Ravitch, Diane. 1985. *The Schools We Deserve: Reflections on the Educational Crises of Our Times*. New York: Basic Books.

Sebba, Judy, and Carol Robinson. 2010. 'Evaluation of UNICEF UK's Rights Respecting Schools Award'. Final Report. University of Brighton.

Commission on Citizenship. 1990. *Encouraging Citizenship: Report of the Commission on Citizenship*. London: H.M. Stationery Office.

Terrorism Act. 2000.

'The Rights Respecting Schools Award Strands - UNICEF UK'. n.d. Rights Respecting Schools Award. Accessed 25 November 2022. https://www.unicef.org.uk/rights-respecting-schools/the-rrsa/the-rrsa-strands/

Select Committee on Citizenship and Civic Engagement, 'The Ties That Bind: Citizenship and Civic Engagement in the 21st Century' or The Ties That Bind. 2018.

Westheimer, Joel, and Joseph Kahne. 2004. 'What Kind of Citizen? The Politics of Educating for Democracy'. *American Educational Research Journal* 41 (2): 237–69.

Wiggan, Jay. 2011. 'Something Old and Blue, or Red, Bold and New? Welfare Reform and the Coalition Government'. In *Social Policy Review 23: Analysis and Debate in Social Policy, 2011*, edited by Chris Holden, Majella Kilkey, and Gaby Ramia, 25–44. Bristol: Policy Press.

Willetts, David. 1994. *Civic Conservatism*. London: Social Market Foundation.

Winch, Christopher. 1998. 'Authority in Education'. In *Encyclopedia of Applied Ethics. Vol. 1: A - D*, edited by Ruth F. Chadwick, 222–28. San Diego, CA: Academic Press.

Wright, Nigel. 1989. *Free School: The White Lion Experience*. Leicestershire: Libertarian Education.

Federated disestablishment of education and state

Introduction

In the first of these two concluding chapters, which represents the first of two positive arguments, I shall propose that the most effective way of minimising institutional coercion from the educational setting is through a state-funded and independent model, one that I call the federated disestablishment of education and state.

I build my position on the foundations, not just of my protagonists Rousseau, Dewey, and Freire but by Amy Gutmann's defence of Federalism that she develops to support her model of democratic education, a model which protects the participants of education, provides for the society they are a part of, and creates checks and measures to mitigate coercive control by families, communities, or the state. However, I reconstruct this model in light of the objections that I raise which draws greater attention to the coercive force of the state.

There are two significant aspects to the institutional arrangement that I propose: federalism and the disestablishment of education and state. These are both very rich and will be addressed, in the first instance, separately. I will then explain how I imagine them together. At the risk of repeating myself, I will state clearly upfront that the propositions that I make in this chapter, as is the case in Chapter 7, and as is the case with my whole positive thesis, are neither designed to be the fixed solution to the tension between the individual and society nor to the problem of authority. The method that I have embraced and attempted to draw out as the central component of this politico-educational thesis is the primary contribution that I wish to make – the conclusions that I express here and in Chapter 7 are the conclusions that I believe are best suited for the realisation of the process in the world in which we live. This is not ideal theory, and short of pressing the reset button we must acknowledge the impossibility of ignoring the means that we employ in achieving the ends for which we strive. To paraphrase the words of the politician Eugene Debs, "I would not lead a person out of bondage even if I could; for if they can be led out, then they could be led back again". It is instead then our responsibility as members

DOI: 10.4324/9781003271871-7

of the world to help ourselves and others develop the tools and skills that we need in order to break out of our bondage together. This is what I believe federalism and the disestablishment of education and state can achieve.

Federalism and the disestablishment of education and state

There are, of course, other ways of decentralising authority as well as federalism. The two most obvious are libertarianism and anarchism. The former I shall refute and the latter remains, in some way, my end-in-view. However, rather than embracing fully the conclusions of my arguments, or maybe because I have paid especial care to them, I do not advocate for anarchism and the dissolution of government apparatus in these pages. To do so, even when all assumptions and arguments lead there, would be the biggest contravention of anarchist principles. It would be the gravest imposition and the most coercive act imaginable. Furthermore, instrumentally, it would be wholly naïve and arrogant to suppose, not just that one person or small group of persons know what is best for all people but that in addressing only the institutional arrangement of society, we will be left with people, as we are, but without the institutional arrangements upon which we have come to depend. Such a violent act, as even the most peaceable dissolution would be, will serve no purpose and achieve no end other than violence in return.

What then must be done in response to the authority imposed upon us, and upon young people in particular, that has not been shown to be legitimate? What institutional solutions are available that do not in turn impose conditions and values on those who have been neither consulted nor enfranchised. While I would want to answer this question more fully, it is beyond the scope of this current enquiry, and I shall satisfy myself by looking specifically at the institutional arrangement of education within an existing state – to do otherwise is too divorced from reality to be valuable. Although it would be fair to assume that I believe the basic position that I outline here to be extendable and encompass the arrangements of the state apparatus as a whole, I will not pursue that here.

Throughout the course of this book, I hope to have shown the problems in the relationship between the individual and society and the consequent problem of authority, and how our existing ideas around education and political structure create unjustified authority relations between people; that these relations are unjustifiable because they are top-down, unilateral, and resistant to change because of the principle of self-preservation; and that this principle becomes undemocratic and coercive in its practice and is most evident in the role that the economy plays in enforcing the status quo. I shall address this at the interactional level in Chapter 7, which I must emphasise is mutually co-dependent upon this chapter and works in concert with and concurrently to the institutional structure of education – the present subject of this chapter.

Let me return to the concepts of federalism and disestablishmentarianism explicitly. These are intended as moderate modifications at the institutional level. They are so because if I were to suggest wide-scale unilateral changes to the institutional setting, then I would need to explain why that does not constitute an illegitimate imposition of value over others, and I could not, because it would be so. My response to the problems that I have identified is also moderate because it is not designed to be the final word on political institutional arrangements, it is but a means to mitigate the most coercive political forces, render them apparent, bring them into political discussion, and subject them to a reflective process. My suggestions then are a starting point by which we move towards a free community of equals and not an expression of freedom as such.

The primary aim is to cultivate a political environment which permits change without arbitrary or illegitimate obstruction to that change, and that the changes proposed originate through discussion with each other and represent the values that those people wish to embody. There is no need for Rawls' Original Position or his reflective equilibrium in a political state of affairs where the political unit has not been trained towards individualism and moral disinterestedness. Similarly, the threat of the Sexual Contract (Pateman 1997) and the Racial Contract (Mills 2011) in the insidious enforcement of the white male worldview under the guise of egalitarianism is minimised by moving the political and moral constructive force away from existing power relations and embedding them in a reflective youth. Although it is important for me to note that as a white male I am not best placed to perceive the validity of this claim, and I must also acknowledge that our prejudices towards others are some of our most deeply embedded blindnesses. As a further aside, this is a pertinent reason why I must be careful of my own authority in the assertion of conclusions that have not included the active voice of others. The hope is that a federalist political structure supported by the disestablishment of education and state will provide the politico-educational space for us, together, to overcome our prejudices and fear of the other – whether that be of people or ideas – and reveal the societies that we wish to be a part of and the ability to build a social environment in that image.

The greatest and most obvious objection to my position as it stands is the worry of violent, hateful, prejudicial, and discriminatory societies being built as a result. There is the further worry that the participants of the process will choose to dissolve said process after establishing the world in their image. My initial response to the first concern is, *unlike what we have?* I do not mean to sound flippant, but the world in which we live has been dragged kicking and screaming towards a forensic equality that we are still some way short of and continues to actively discriminate, bully, harass, and obfuscate in response to the continued struggle for the realisation of the freedom and equality promised. Maybe the worry is that the method that I propose will bring about something worse; however, I fear that this is simply a symptom of our dominating fear of change. This response will not make the worry any less so and is not an adequate response on its own. Therefore, it is also important to note that this is one of the great advantages of federalism as opposed to a direct move into anarchism. It provides structural support for a people not yet ready for the freedom of anarchism, for a people who are still led by fear and prejudice, but without resorting to the fictions hypothesised by Rousseau or the epistemic authority of teachers employed by Dewey and Freire. In the following section, I shall answer the concern more fully and lay out in more detail the role that federalism plays within this institutional argument, but first, and to conclude this section, I shall note once more that these fears are why the institutional response to the tension between the individual and society must be sought in concert with and concurrently to an interactional structure of education which promotes the development of the person. Without this pairing either branch of enquiry could certainly result in a great perversion of humanity.

The definition and form of federalism

Federalism is a political theory which divides the power of the state between member units. It is a method by which power is non-centralised because it is shared between at least two levels of governance. This is not a new idea; the United States is a federalist nation which is composed of the national government and the governments of each individual state. Traditionally, the role of the president was focussed on foreign affairs, the role of Congress was focussed on national affairs, and the states had the authority to govern themselves otherwise independently of the political whole. Elements of UK politics are also federalist in some ways, especially since the establishment of the devolved governments of Scotland, Northern Ireland, and Wales. Furthermore, a number of other countries also identify their government as federalist in structure, including Argentina, Belgium, Brazil, Ethiopia, and Mexico.

Amy Gutmann, in *Democratic Education*, to which I keep returning for good reason, defended federalism as the governmental structure needed to balance the competing interests, in the education system of the United States, of parents and the state. Gutmann develops an argument in favour of democratic education but accepts that democracy must be limited to a certain degree because otherwise one can find the results of democratic deliberation being contrary to the values of democracy. For example, the favouring of one group of people over another or the prohibition of certain beliefs or practices. Guttmann writes, "Democratic control over primary schools is worth defending, but not if its results are repressive or discriminatory" (1999, 71). It is Gutmann's aim to provide a framework for educational institutions and not the answer to the particular problems of those institutions.

According to Gutmann, a democratic theory of education provides the best structure for finding that answer. This is because, as opposed to alternative theories of education, a democratic theory of education can provide principles that work in concert with our tendency to disagree. Gutmann writes, "A democratic theory of education provides principles that, in the face of our social disagreements, help us judge (a) who should have the authority to make decisions about education, and (b) what the moral boundaries of that authority are" (1999, 11).

Gutmann defends this delicate position by sketching an example in the shape of a small independent city-state. This state has a national identity, which is a part of the citizens' social identity. The citizens also have particular identities, for example, their religion, ethnicity, occupation, and familial and friendship groups. As such, the state has one universal and a multitude of particular identities. It is Gutmann's belief that it is the role of education to, "aid in shaping the social identity of future citizens by cultivating or changing common culture" (Gutmann 1999, 72). This common culture has two parts: first, those things particular to any one society and, second, those things determined to be essential to any democratic state. Democratic control of education can only support the first part of common culture. According to Gutmann, the second part of common culture, those principles which are shared amongst all democratic societies, or ought to be shared by all people, is not adequately protected by democratic practice. Therefore, principles that Gutmann broadly conceives of as principles of nondiscrimination and nonrepression are protected by the state and sit outside of any democratic deliberation, and as such, principled constraints on democratic authority are justifiably exercised.

With this in mind, within the limits of her hypothesised small independent city-state, Gutmann believes that a school board, held accountable for their policies by voters, would be the ideal of democratic education, provided that the school board does not violate the principles of nonrepression and nondiscrimination. Gutmann believes that this works because the, "lines of accountability are so short and clearly drawn", but school politics must remain, "competitive and conducive to public deliberation, so that school board members do not defer as a matter of course to the administrators of schools" (Gutmann 1999, 73). However, in a larger society, it becomes more complicated. If things are left in complete local control, then the society is divided into a collection of city-states with no interest in a common education. If education becomes centralised within the national government, then democracy is eliminated.

Gutmann's model of democratic education aims to find the balance between the competing institutional authorities. She motivates her answer in a synthesis of three normative theories of education as explicated by Plato, John Locke, and John Stuart Mill. According to Gutmann, the authority of each of these normative theories is, respectively, the state as guardian, the family as guardian, and no guardian without assurance of children's interests being primary. Gutmann believes that none of these theories hold but that each authority defended in these theories must have an element of control to create balance. The state must protect the value of democracy, the parents must protect the values of their home, and the professional autonomy of the teachers must protect the objective interests of the children themselves (Gutmann 1999, 41–42). This represents the foundation of her federalist model of democratic education.

Gutmann considers the multiple levels of democratic authority over schools and then the role of the teachers as a part of that democratic system. Gutmann then considers the effects of these authorities on the children within the compulsory education system and what room there is for them to have a say in shaping their schooling. Gutmann perceives three levels of legitimate democratic authority over schools: the federal, the state, and the local. The question of the degree of control for each level is, as Gutmann writes, "an issue of enormous complexity" (1999, 77). However, it is a balance that is to be found through federalism and not a promotion of any one of these authorities over the others.

Federalism protects and promotes democracy at a local level and limits the authority of that local power only in regard to, "the aims of cultivating a common culture and teaching essential democratic values" (Gutmann 1999, 74). The difficulty for Gutmann is to have a balance of power that protects the essential values of democracy at all levels, cultivates the common culture at all levels, but allows for the local level to, "remain free to set their own standards, as well as to use their discretion in deciding how to implement federal and state decisions" (Gutmann 1999, 74). Gutmann does not attempt to draw out the lines of power in more detail. The point that she wishes to make is that in a large society, there are several levels of legitimate authority, but the local level should not be undermined by the powers above them, only facilitated and protected.

Gutmann's educational structure has a federal democratic power that protects the values of democracy with principles of nondiscrimination and nonrepression. Below that there is the "state" level of democracy that promotes those values that are particular to that "state". Examples of this could be the protection and promotion of a local language or dialect, but it is limited in its scope by the principles of nondiscrimination and nonrepression that are established at the national level and outside of the democratic process. Below that is the locally elected school board who set the standards of education limited only by those essential characteristics dictated by the authorities above them. This terminology does not translate perfectly into the context of politics in the United Kingdom but can be loosely mapped over to apply first to the state, then to the nations of the United Kingdom, and lastly to the councils, boroughs, and metropolitan districts, etc., that comprise our local political authorities.

Nondemocratic groups also play a very important role in Gutmann's federated model of democratic education. Without proper and legitimate challenges to the authority of the majority as represented at federal, state, and local levels, there will remain the risk of the status quo becoming staid and oppressive. According to Gutmann, nondemocratic pressure groups are essential in challenging the status quo and helping to shape educational policy. The most important of these are the teachers and teachers' unions. The role that Gutmann believes teachers should play is one that cultivates their students' capacity for critical reflection on the common culture at local, state, and federal levels. Through the professional expertise of the teachers, this cultivation is seen to complement the popularity of the democratic authorities who will be perpetuating a common culture. This is how Gutmann addresses what I have identified as the principle of self-preservation in the institutional environment. Where the existing power relations seek to maintain and perpetuate existing values and dominant views of a shared social identity, the teachers and teachers' unions seek to challenge them on behalf of young people and professional best practice. Gutmann writes, "The professional responsibility of teachers is to uphold the principle of nonrepression by cultivating the capacity for democratic deliberation" (1999, 76). Gutmann uses the term "professional" in a particular way. To be a professional, or to practice professionalism, is to be understood as to possess the degree of autonomy "necessary to fulfil the democratic functions of office" (Gutmann 1999, 77). If teachers do not have enough autonomy, then they are at risk of suffering from the ossification of office. If teachers have too much autonomy, then they are at risk of suffering from the insolence of office. We will see the potential risks of this in Chapter 7.

Gutmann's proposal is for a structure of education that is a finely balanced federalist system supported by, and challenged by, the professional authority of teachers on behalf of professional standards and the interests of young people. This structure has definite advantages; the federalist system is well placed to protect the values of democracy as well as the values that are particular to increasingly localised areas, but it places no democracy within the schools themselves, granting only the teachers the authority to legitimately challenge the edicts of the democratic system.

There is a lot that I feel great affinity for in Gutmann's analysis. I believe that she is correct that a federal system of democratic education provides the best framework to cultivate the values and virtues that we believe are essential to our respective cultures and communities. Further to this, I believe that it is the best model for guaranteeing that certain standards, principles, and practices are followed through legislation and enforced by democracy and special interest pressure groups, such as trade unions. However, I think it is clear that Gutmann has underestimated the importance of the practice of democracy in inculcating those democratic virtues. The reason that Gutmann places so little importance on young people practising democracy within their school originates, I believe, from two assumptions, both of which I reject. First, Gutmann professes that the aim or end of education is to create good citizens, and second, that the way to successfully inculcate democratic virtues in children is through ruling over them.

In Chapter 7, I will address this latter assumption and express my concerns with regard to the role of young people in their democratic education within Gutmann's model and respond to her by defending an internally democratic schooling model. In the following section, I shall address the model and scope of the citizen that Gutmann conceives of as the aim of her democratic education. This will raise two key objections to Gutmann and form the foundation of the federated disestablishment of education and state that I defend in this chapter. My first objection is the form that the citizen takes in contrast to the Critical Citizen that I have outlined in Chapter 2 of this book, and the second objection is how that citizen comes to be within a democratic education.

Federalism following Amy Gutmann

Gutmann's citizen is one who holds democratic virtues and who has the ability and self-governance necessary to challenge authority and seek change, both within their local social environment and the state and federal levels of governance. It is clear, however, that Gutmann does not perceive there to be much change forthcoming or that democracy itself might be a part of the reflection of citizens. She writes, "we might better understand the democratic ideal as that of conscious social reproduction, the same ideal that guides democratic education" (1999, 289), but conscious social reproduction is not quite as limiting as it sounds. It is instead, "the ways in which citizens are or should be empowered to influence the education that in turn shapes the political values, attitudes, and modes of behaviour of future citizens" (Gutmann 1999, 14).

The key difference between Gutmann's aim of education and the one that I have shaped in Chapter 2 then is that Gutmann perceives the citizen as a person who possesses the values promoted by those who rule, these values pass down from generation to generation, the citizen inherits the values of our forebears and then they change them for the generation to come, who then in turn modify them. What this, of course, means is that the change that occurs does so less for those that desire it and more for those that it is imposed upon. Further to this, the citizen whom Gutmann believes is best suited as a participant in deliberative democracy is not the citizen who represents her aim of democratic education – it is a more limited goal.

Gutmann employs the three-stage theory of moral development developed by John Rawls to illustrate the aim of her democratic model. In *Theory of Justice*, Rawls sketches out, "the course of moral development as it might occur in a well-ordered society realising the principles of justice as fairness" (1999, 404). He distinguishes between the morality of authority, of association, and of principles in his account of the development of morality. The morality of authority is the first stage of moral development and the one that Rawls equates with the morality of a child. Rawls writes, "it is not characteristic of the child's situation that he is not in a position to assess the validity of the precepts and injunctions addressed to him by those in authority, in this case his parents" (1999, 405). Rawls applies this concept of morality on those who do not have the concept of justification and who lack the knowledge and understanding to be able to make their own judgements.

The second stage of moral development is the morality of association. This is the morality we develop and associate with as a result of those groups to which we belong and identify. It can refer to the family unit, a group with which one identifies, the community of which one is a part, the morality of one's nation, or even one's state. Rawls writes, "the content of the morality of association is given by the moral standards appropriate to the individual's role in the various associations to which he belongs" (1999, 409).

The morality of principles is the third stage of moral development and is when a person attaches their moral outlook to the principles themselves rather than through the associations to which one belongs. Rawls writes, "The conception of acting justly, and of advancing just institutions, comes to have for him an attraction analogous to that possessed before by subordinate levels" (1999, 414). This moral autonomy Gutmann defines as, "the desire and capacity to make moral choices based on principles that are generalizable among all persons" (1999, 59) and a little later on as, "doing what is right and good *because* it is right and good and not because teachers or any other authorities demand it" (1999, 62). This presents moral autonomy in quite a strict, Kantian manner.

However, Gutmann pulls short in her search for an educational framework to strengthen and sustain liberal democracy by not seeking autonomy but rather Rawls' second stage of morality – the morality of association. According to Gutmann, if one attempts to teach morality of principle, they have set their sights too high. Autonomy is not an achievable aim of education. As such, we should forsake any attempt to teach it in favour of the morality of association and limit teaching to the democratic virtues as Gutmann understands them.

According to Gutmann, if we understand virtue as *democratic* virtue, then the schooling system can have much success by teaching through practice. Gutmann believes that democratic virtue can be learnt through the practice of the principles of democracy, i.e. respect of the opinions and background of others. It is because of her interactional commitments that Gutmann stops short of the morality of principle as an aim of education. I believe that Gutmann reaches this conclusion because of a relatively traditional view of "teaching" as a practice. We see a presentation of teaching as something almost unilateral, where a group of people with knowledge share that knowledge with another group who previously lacked this knowledge. In understanding teaching and the teaching environment in such a limited way, Gutmann does not have the framework necessary to imagine anything other than one where there is very little opportunity to practice and challenge the authority of the teacher and the mandates that they issue.

Within Gutmann's limited teaching framework, a problem is created with respect to teaching autonomy. If one aims to teach autonomy within this teaching relationship, one is aiming to teach something that they are not practising, thereby creating a disconnect between the means employed and ends that are desired. This is a problem because it aims to teach something that it does not practice. It aims to teach autonomy that contains within it the principle of self-discovery, while removing that opportunity to develop through self-discovery. It is the equivalent of memorising the answers rather than understanding how those answers were reached. Gutmann writes, "in order to create sovereign citizens, ... [the teacher] must remove one of the most important political decisions from democratic control—the education of future citizens" (1999, 63).

From this position, Gutmann argues that the authority which attempts to teach the morality of principle undermines its own position by being undemocratic but teaching the ideals of autonomous individuals within a democratic society. She writes, "by using nondemocratic means to achieve the end of democratic self-government, ... [the teacher] may teach a lesson incompatible with the assumption of popular sovereignty upon which its authority supposedly rests" (1999, 63–64). In the case of this example, Gutmann believes that we have a choice between our assumption that the most legitimate system of education is that which provides the best results and our belief that the system of democratic education is the best foundation for our moral education. The former requires two further assumptions: first that educators have the capacity and knowledge to teach the whole of virtue, and second, that we can rely upon those educators to teach it. These assumptions are not easily digested and arguably implausible. As such, Gutmann argues, we should choose democratic rationale. Gutmann writes, "The price of denying democratic authority over schools is dispensing with the democratic purposes of primary education" (1999, 64).

In aiming for the morality of association, Gutmann sets herself apart from most proponents of the social-justice-oriented citizen and certainly distinguishes herself from the aims of Rousseau, Dewey, and Freire. The morality of association is akin to the Sovereign of the republic before it has learnt to determine the General Will and is still dependent on the mandates of the Lawgiver and the morality of given religion. Their vision of what the autonomous person looks like may differ, and they may disagree on how to achieve their respective visions, but what they share is a commitment to the full realisation of the free individual through education. However, we need not accept Gutmann's negative conclusion. A mistake is made in pulling short of the morality of principle as an aim of education. In Chapter 7, I shall argue that it can be achieved through another feature which Gutmann rejects too quickly, that of internally democratic schools. In the following section, however, I shall address my second objection to Gutmann – her failure to adequately account for the coercive power of the state and its role in forming the citizen.

Coercion from economic forces

My second major objection to Amy Gutmann is that she permits too great an influence of the state over the model of education and the form of the citizen. This is a complaint that is shared with libertarians who argue for the removal of state influence from the schooling system. I explored their arguments in detail in Chapter 4 in reference to their opposition to democratic education and their response to Gutmann. In short, the objection is that if the state has authority over the content of education and the values taught in education settings, then they will teach that which perpetuates a state like them. There is a great coercive power of the state, and by allowing the state too great a control over education, that coercion will aim to eliminate competing worldviews through assimilation, integration, or violence.

Gutmann recognises the importance of limiting the authority of the state in the education of its citizens. This is what her federal model of democratic education is designed to overcome. The national government has power only to enforce principles of nondiscrimination and nonrepression in education. However, this is insufficient according to the libertarian theorist, and there persists an unjustifiable coercion that imposes itself in the education setting. McConnell thinks that Gutmann's conception of the citizen is too thick. Indeed, as noted in Chapter 4, according to McConnell, to find a conception of the citizen that is agreeable to all is to find a conception of the citizen that is trivial or meaningless. But more than this, McConnell believes that families are better placed to choose the educational philosophy of their children in a similar manner to how the families are allowed to choose their religion. He is critical of Gutmann because, "the democratic argument fails to recognise the particular problem posed for families whose understanding of 'educational aims' includes the idea that religious faith is an essential aspect of education, which should be integrated into the curriculum" (McConnell 2002, 100).

In contrast to McConnell highlighting of the coercive power of the state, there is the egalitarianism of Illich and Reimer. In the eyes of these two radical educators, formal schooling is a barrier to learning. Illich drew an important distinction between schooling and learning. The former, when funded and run by the state, was necessarily a venue of insidious training and belief formation. Reimer, similarly, argues that school is a system that maintains the existing oppressive state of affairs and assists only in deepening the inequalities that separate us.

I do not think that Gutmann can adequately respond to the concerns raised by this anti-state education coalition. The imposition of the state in education is therefore unjustifiable because of its inherent imposition on freedom. However, Friedman and McConnell are guilty of an even greater oversight in their analysis than Gutmann. They have achieved nothing in moving the sight of oppressive action from the national government and placing it within the home. No persuasive argument can been made to support the assumption that parents' rights should consistently trump the rights of the child. It may be the case that Gutmann failed in creating a legitimate balance of powers between the state and the family home, but it is a stronger theory than one that argues in favour of placing young people wholly under the yoke of a different power. Neither side in this argument has given adequate attention to the rights of the young people themselves – the voice that they must be provided in an environment of competing rulers. McConnell leans heavily on the dis-analogy that he makes between the freedom to practise religion and the prescribed democratic citizen that operates as Gutmann's aim of education. McConnell, much like Gutmann, treats those subject to education as voiceless passengers. Where Gutmann subordinates them to the liberal democratic state, McConnell subordinates them to the will of their family elders. I will turn to this question in Chapter 7, but there is another and more troubling objection that I hold against, not just Gutmann and the libertarians but also the egalitarians Illich and Reimer. It is the failure to adequately consider and comprehend the coercive force of the market and its relation to education.

Where the existence of significant state coercion leads writers like Friedman, McConnell, Illich, and Reimer to look towards free market capitalism in some form or another for the solution to that control, Clive Erricker argues that the coercion of the state over its subjects is currently being fuelled by that economic perspective. According to Erricker, free market capitalism is not the solution but the cause.

Erricker, in a similar vein to Freidman, McConnell, Illich, and Reimer, perceives unjustifiable constraints on the subjects of education when it is controlled by the state. However, Erricker sees the conflation of the values of democracy with the interests of free market capitalism as a major source of the coercion that takes place. He writes,

> Government pronouncements on family values, parenting, education, citizenship and many other matters seek to convince us that democratic ideals shape the changes that are taking place in these areas and that our society will become more democratic as a result.
>
> (2002, iv)

Erricker says that this is not the case. It is a subterfuge that is to be designed to convince us of the unification of the interests of democracy and free market capitalism. According to Erricker, there is no balance between these two forces. He argues that the force of capitalism is dominant and that the values of democracy bend to fit within the free market. He writes, "The result is a cosmetic veneer of democratic rhetoric used to justify economically anti-democratic practices" (2002, iv).

This is an important argument because Erricker agrees with McConnell and Freidman that the states' involvement in schooling is a coercive and unjustifiable constraint on freedom. Further, he agrees with Illich and Reimer that the school environment is not one that cultivates equality and opportunity. However, Erricker sees the problems through a different lens. He writes,

> Despite claims to the contrary, that insist that the school is a place of opportunity for learners, it is not. The children are there for the teacher, the teacher is there to carry out the requirements of the centralised agencies, the centralised agencies are there to implement government policy, government policy aims to create wealth. The schools and the children are there to serve the government in this aim, everything else is subservient to this.
>
> (2002, 48)

Schools do perpetuate the existing power relations and government does exert undue coercion in education, according to Erricker, but it is not to be understood solely in terms of the imposition of the values of the liberal democratic state. No, the root of the coercion in Erricker's view is the subservience of the liberal democratic state to undemocratic economic forces.

Erricker draws out the coercive force of the economy on individuals and the power that exerts across society. He argues that if we understand the free capitalist market as one which satisfies demand, then we must acknowledge that it does not draw a distinction between needs, wants, and desires. Then, it must be conceded that if wants and desires produce a greater demand, then the market will provide for those above needs. If society is one with unequal power relations and the interests of the wealthy sufficiently outweigh the interests of the poor, then the market will satisfy the demands of want from the wealthy above the interests of need from the poor. Erricker writes, "within an economy that creates wealth inequality. Increasingly, it provides for the prosperous, thus, over and above the basic needs we all have, it seeks to create a market for the consumption of the prosperous: a market of luxuries" (2002, 40).

This structure of power and form of the economy is inculcated and normalised in schools. They form the foundation of the values that are taught and delivered as being in the interests of all. Erricker notes, "The values within the school act as a form of social control that works well for those who conform and succeed but pushes those who do not into situations of docile acceptance, punishment or even exclusion" (2002, 55).

In this way, Erricker's argument runs counter to all of those discussed so far in this section. He argues that the consequence of privatisation is not increased parental choice, individual liberty, or equality because free market capitalism has the ability to limit the options of the poor just as it increases available options for those with the means to take advantage of them. The market affects options through things such as rising house prices in good school neighbourhoods and the disproportionate weight paid to the interests of the wealthy by the market. Therefore, according to Erricker, "schooling replicates the effects of the free-market economy, even if a system of parental choice is not operated" (2002, 55).

Erricker therefore differs from those above because he recognises the coercive impact of the economy on freedom, equality, and education as well as the state. He writes, "Our society is not served by, and our institutions are collapsing under, the weight of government regulation and the impetus to de-regulation in the economic world. What is happening in schools and higher education institutions is symptomatic of this" (2002, 65).

Those, like Friedman, McConnell, Illich, and Reimer, who shift authority into the private economic sphere through a policy of disestablishment argue persuasively against state influence in education. James Tooley makes similar arguments to McConnell in favour of the privatisation of education through disestablishment from the state (Tooley 1996, 2000, 2017). However, their solutions are bemusing. McConnell argues that education is the primary method of the state to inculcate the values and character of the citizen. He writes, "We depend on elementary and secondary schools to inculcate the values and ideals necessary for the next generation to become responsible citizens in our democratic society" (2002, 94). This fits with the intention of Rousseau's institutional structure of education where a civil religion transmitted through the Lawgiver to the Sovereign defines and develops the character of the citizen, and it suffers from the same objection of insidious and manipulative control. McConnell attributes this view to Gutmann and to the present US Supreme Court (McConnell cites, Arnbach v. Norwick, 441 U.S. 68 in support of this charge of the US Supreme Court). In the United Kingdom, a similar point can be made with the current application of fundamental British values, the prevent strategy, the existing curriculum, and the National Citizenship Service (NCS) discussed above. Also, the recent select committee, *The Ties that Bind*, discussed above supports this view, at one point it reads, "we have found that citizenship education, … should be the first great opportunity for instilling and developing our values, encouraging social cohesion, and creating active citizens" (*The Ties That Bind* 2018, 4). This imposition is unjustified, according to McConnell, not because it is inherently coercive as the deschoolers argue, but because it is coercive on those who think otherwise and wish to raise their children by other standards, with other values, and to possess a different character. This is most obvious in the case of religion. McConnell writes,

> Collective judgements about the ideological and philosophical content of the curriculum must be made; dissenters as well as believers will be forced to pay for it; and dissenters must either allow their children to be educated according to precepts they dispute or finance the alternative from their own resources. This is an inherently coercive arrangement, seemingly at odds with liberal principle.
>
> (2002, 104)

As mentioned above, McConnell's resolution to this tension is publicly funded private education through state-issued vouchers. He raises the point that even with this minimal role, the state retains the power to exercise some coercion. Noting that, "It may be objected that ... the role of financing and of quality control—carries dangers of the establishment of orthodoxy. The power to deny accreditation to schools could indeed be used as a weapon against dissenting viewpoints" (McConnell 2002, 104–105). Yet, at no point does McConnell consider the coercive force of private industry. The coercive power of the state is seen with such clarity, but on the coercive power of the economy, McConnell is silent. How can this be so? While the market may be free in the libertarian formulation, those subject to the market, as Erricker persuasively argues, are not. In a free market, companies have an obligation to make profits for their shareholders. This subordinates the interests of non-shareholders to the shareholders. Yet, the most significant difference between the market and the democratic state is that the former is not subject to checks and measures, and it is not subject to the voice of the people. It is an undemocratic institution that trades on its freedom as a justification for the coercion that every person suffers as a result of its ebb and flow.

I do not argue in favour of any form of private education, nor do I support the privatisation of schools through the academisation process in the United Kingdom. The umbrella companies that own the academy institutions are often for-profit organisations, and they therefore cannot hold the interests of the students as primary. Nothing subject to the market and economic interest can ever be in the interests of the world's poor. It is my view that neither privately financed nor publicly controlled education serves the interests of the people who are educated. In the former, the interests of the economy must be primary, and the individuals educated are tools for the furtherance of those who benefit from the economy. In the latter, the interests of the state are primary, and the individuals educated are tools for the furtherance of the values of that state.

Conclusion

The federated disestablishment of education and state that I imagine is informed largely by Gutmann's federalist model of democratic education. Where I differ from Gutmann is in the spheres of democracy that constitute the federalism, the role of young people in the formation and practice of their education, and the method by which the model of the citizen emerges within that democratic model.

The institutional model that I defend is that which is best placed to respond to the problem of authority and find that balance in the tension between the individual and society. It is also informed by the destructive thesis of those that perceive the coercive nature of institutional bodies, such as the state and the economy. These are powers over the individual that, especially in large and complex societies, are difficult to hold accountable for their actions and place adequate checks and measures upon to protect the citizens subject to their rules and actions. I take it as a given that just like the person who clung fast to their coat as the wind blew, the state and the economy if threatened will cling fast to their power. There is no sudden or violent resolution to the coercion that persists.

Therefore, key to the institutional structure of education is that the citizen is defined, discovered, and embodied by those of each generation. A bottom-up construct of federalism that is constructed in such a way that the voice of each is valued and the values of each inform the democracy they participate in. In my conclusion to this book, I shall humour my imagination and propose how I perceive this model will look in practice when it is accompanied by the interactional structure of education that is the subject of Chapter 7.

References

Erricker, Clive. 2002. *When Learning Becomes Your Enemy: The Relationship Between Education, Spiritual Dissent and Economics*. Nottingham: Educational Heretics Press.

Gutmann, Amy. 1999. *Democratic Education*. Princeton, NJ; Chichester: Princeton University Press.

McConnell, Michael W. 2002. 'Education Disestablishment: Why Democratic Values Are Ill-Served by Democratic Control of Schooling'. In *Moral and Political Education*, edited by Stephen Macedo and Yael Tamir, 87–146. Nomos, XLIII. New York: New York University Press.

Mills, Charles W. 2011. *The Racial Contract*. Nachdr. Ithaca, NY: Cornell University Press.

Pateman, Carole. 1997. *The Sexual Contract*. Reprint. Cambridge: Polity Press.

Rawls, John. 1999. *A Theory of Justice*. Rev. ed. Cambridge, MA: Belknap Press of Harvard University Press.

Select Committee on Citizenship and Civic Engagement, 'The Ties That Bind: Citizenship and Civic Engagement in the 21st Century' or The Ties That Bind. 2018.

Tooley, James. 1996. *Education Without the State.* IEA Studies in Education 1. London: IEA Education and Training Unit.

Tooley, James. 2000. *Reclaiming Education.* London; New York: Cassell.

Tooley, James. 2017. *Disestablishing the School: De-Bunking Justifications for State Intervention in Education.* London; New York: Taylor & Francis.

Chapter 7

Internally democratic schooling

Introduction

Complementing the federated disestablishment of education and state are a body of internally democratic schools – the form of which I will explore in this chapter. I will return to Summerhill and look at how democracy is practised inside its domain and how its pedagogical practice supports their democracy. I will then look in more detail at the free school movement and their attempts to bring the principles of progressive education and internally democratic schooling out of the secluded world of the independent school and into the realm of state-funded education. Once I have introduced the principles and practices of the internally democratic school, I shall explore potential objections to them. I shall attempt to respond to these concerns and explain how the internally democratic school answers the questions raised in this book as a whole, namely the tension between the individual and society, the problem of authority, and the realisation of the Critical Citizen.

I then argue that there remains a more significant problem that has lain hidden in an assumed characteristic of all previous conceptualisations of authority. This ontological assumption is responsible for the otherwise irresolvable conflict between authority and freedom. In reconceiving authority as a relational property rather than a unilateral one that is expressed from one person or group over another person of group, the barriers to an effective model of internally democratic schooling are lifted, and it is incorporated into the federated disestablishment of education and state providing a bottom-up democracy with education at its heart and the Critical Citizen as its aim.

Exploring the internally democratic school

I introduced the principles that underpinned the practice of Summerhill school in Chapter 5; however, it is worth returning to them here because democracy has always been a central feature of the school since its institution. As noted previously, at Summerhill freedom is the primary value. For a child to be free, the adult must remove their authority, refrain from the teaching of right and wrong, cease projecting their own repression and hate onto the

DOI: 10.4324/9781003271871-8

child, and allow the child the same rights and freedoms as any adult. These concerns define the institutional structure of the school. For example, at Summerhill, there is no room inspection, and no one will clean the rooms on behalf of the young people; there is no uniform, each child being free to wear what they choose; one is not obligated to attend class; there are no examinations; the staff and the pupils eat the same food and obey the same community laws; the rules and regulations of the school are determined by democratic discussion and vote, and punishments for transgression of those rules and regulations are dealt with in a similar manner. At Summerhill, there is a concerted effort to remove the domination of child by adult; there is no head of power, no authority figure, and no ruler and ruled.

This system of democratic self-governance, alongside the active removal of adult authority, is justified by Neill's analysis of the psychology of the child discussed in Chapter 5. But to briefly repeat myself, the imposition of one worldview, presented as right and true when it represents in reality just one of countless manifestations of a reasonably stable way of life, causes anxiety and self-hatred in a child when their desires run up against these imposed values. This hatred is directed internally and externally, and teaches children that they are wrong or bad for feeling otherwise. Furthermore, imposing authority on young people imposes limits on their ability to think for themselves. Therefore, for the well-being of the psychology of young people, education must teach them instead how to be self-governing and autonomous and must be designers of the world in which they wish to live. If followed through this leads to an internally democratic structure of the school.

The relationships between members of the school community are defined by democratic practice. The rules, regulations, and punishments are all discussed and decided upon democratically during the weekly General School Meeting (GSM). At the start of term, a chairman is elected, and the reigning chairman appoints their successor for the next week. Each pupil and each teacher participate in the GSM, and every person has one vote. Neill writes,

> In Summerhill, everyone has equal rights. No one is allowed to walk on my grand piano, and I am not allowed to borrow a boy's cycle without his permission. At a General School Meeting, the vote of a child of six counts for as much as my vote does.
>
> (1968, 24)

Motions are carried on a strict majority rule. This is true of rules passed as well as when alleged infringements of those rules are considered. The people of the school act as executive, legislature, and judiciary. Neill's educational model provides an institutional structure for the development of self-governing individuals but does not illustrate how this can be achieved within the classroom. The theory and practice of teaching was not a concern for Neill because, in his view, all a child needed was the desire to learn which is what the structure of his school provided. As a result, while Neill was the master of the school, the lessons remained didactic and rote.

Neill's Summerhill is an example of one half of the progressive education movement in the United Kingdom, the independent progressive school. In the United Kingdom, inspired by educators such as Neill, the 1960s and 1970s saw an attempt to bring the principles of Summerhill out of the small world of independent schools and make it accessible to all. This is often characterised as the free school movement.[1] Nigel Wright identifies three ways in which free schools were free. They were monetarily free to attend, they were free of the influence of the state and church, and they practised a model of education designed to maximise individual freedom for the children (Wright 1989a, 93). Wright worked at White Lion Street Free School for four years and concentrated on that school in offering a critical examination of the theory and practice behind the free school movement. Schools such as White Lion Street aimed to employ some of the principles of the progressive independent schools such as Summerhill but without the barriers of fees. Wright quotes a passage from the school's first bulletin.

> The children will be free to learn what they want to learn – so long as it does not interfere with anyone else. It will be their decision, in the first place, that they want to come to the school … They will also have an equal say with the adults in how the school is run. Most children want to learn. Not only useful things like reading and writing, but also how the world – as they see it – works. But they cannot learn if they are forced to do it from lessons which have no connection with the lives they lead after school.
>
> (Wright 1989b, ix)

At White Lion Street School, there was, "No divisional office, no head-teacher, no hierarchy, no compulsory curriculum, no reactionary colleagues, no need to submit to other people's constraints" (Wright 1989b, ix). However, while a structure like this appears to have aimed at the complete abolition of authority, a closer examination shows that authority has simply been recalibrated. Decisions made by the school were made in two weekly meetings which were open to all children and parents as well as the workers. Wright writes, "For [White Lion Street School], democracy was at the centre of its philosophy. All members of the school community – children, parents and workers – were invited to take an equal part in decision making" (1989b, 12).

In these internally democratic schools, the practice of free action and thought by the students can be harnessed to build a democratic structure in the image of the values discovered by the students through dialogue with each other. The internally democratic school emphasises the voice of the student and puts it into conversation with the state, community, school, and family. However, they were not without forms of control.

In spite of their commitment to freedom, the workers exercised some form of interventionist role (Wright 1989b, 32). Wright illustrates the tension between the freedom of the child and the authority of the adult that was present in the White Lion Street School in his discussion on nagging. He writes, "'Nagging' was the technique used by WL [White Lion Street] workers to get children to do things (or refrain from doing things) whilst pretending that the children were free to do otherwise" (1989b, 33). Therefore, authority persisted at White Lion Street School in various forms: there was the authority of the workers in nagging and interfering; there was the authority of the democratic system; and there was also the authority of the "stooges", as they were referred to, who were the owners of and fundraisers for the school.

Wright is honest about his experiences at White Lion Street School and explains the problems they had in participation and engagement in the democratic system and in protecting the values that underpinned it from potentially damaging decisions. It seems clear in Wright's analysis that White Lion Street School struggled with maintaining a consistency to its values and philosophy. However, Wright also tells of the beauty and the success, of the times when the children were active, reflective, and committed to working together to find resolution and consensus. He notes that the destructiveness of some was not the norm. There were other children who did use their freedom constructively (Wright 1989b, 29). Speaking of the more positive aspects of White Lion Street School, Wright focuses on a few particular practices which stood them apart from the regular comprehensive school system. One of these differences was in the nature and form of the relationships between the children and the workers. "WL [White Lion Street School] went some way towards breaking free of these institutional constraints and putting relationships back into the 'personal sphere'" (Wright 1989b, 51). At White Lion Street School, there was a great deal of physical contact between adults and children. Wright attributes the strong relationships borne out of this tactile relationship an instrumental value, and to many of the successes at the school. He writes,

> Although there were exceptions, WL [White Lion Street School] found that it was the children with whom workers had the closest, most open relationships who got most out of the school. They, in the main, were the ones who took a responsible part in the democratic process, who made constructive use of the school's freedoms, who took advantage of learning opportunities.
>
> (1989b, 51)

These successes do not answer the problems of nagging, bullying, and disengagement that Wright highlights within White Lion Street School, and there are further problems with internally democratic schooling. In the next section, I shall consider some of the stronger objections before responding to them all later in this chapter.

Objections to internally democratic schooling

Within the United Kingdom at least, the free school movement marks the high-water mark of progressive education and internally democratic schooling. There has been since a slow but inexorable shift away from the principles that defined progressive practice and were enshrined in law following the Plowden Report in 1967. A report that was largely influenced by the theory of John Dewey. Presently in government and the Department of Education, there are few defenders of the progressive ideals that are exemplified by Summerhill school, and the democratic voice of young people is largely ignored, even by those who characterise themselves as proponents of democratic education.

One of those people is Amy Gutmann who makes three objections to "overly" internally democratic schools – two direct objections and a third indirect objection (Gutmann 1999, 77). First, Gutmann claims that the success of internally democratic schools is, at least in part, due to the fact that they practise selective enrolment, and therefore, their methods are not implementable on a larger scale. Gutmann argues that those schools which give students equal control often practise a student selection process and predefined intent that results in the children that frequent their schools being predisposed towards the philosophy espoused. The selective enrolment practised by those schools therefore gives a bias result. This policy, Gutmann believes, is impractical in state-funded education because in state-funded education, difficult students may challenge the democratic conception of teaching "because" of their attitude, thereby encouraging the teacher to become increasingly authoritarian (Gutmann 1999, 77). The inevitability of difficult students in a state school encourages authoritarian action and undermines any democracy.

Second, Gutmann believes that children are not capable of making the right decisions for themselves and that if children are given this power that the teacher has ceded their professional autonomy. Gutmann dismisses the role of young people themselves in playing a democratic role within their education. Following Aristotle, Gutmann declares, "being educated as a child entails being ruled" and continues, "Because being a democratic citizen entails ruling, the ideal of democratic education is being ruled, then ruling" (1999, 3). Although Gutmann is sympathetic to increased participation by children in many decisions that directly affect their schooling, "The solution", she writes, "… cannot be to give students equal control over the conditions of their schooling" (1999, 88). This is because the students do not possess the skills necessary to be directly involved in decision-making at school. Gutmann notes that children can be immature, self-centred, and lack the life experience that give adults invaluable powers of reflection and empathy.

The third objection that Gutmann makes is that because of the educational practices of schools such as Summerhill, there is a distinct risk of teachers developing what she calls the "insolence of office" (Gutmann 1999, 77). This is the strongest argument that Gutmann develops when considering schools such as Summerhill, but it was not one that was levelled directly at internally democratic schools. In discussing the ideal structure of compulsory education, Gutmann writes about the potential of teachers' suffering from the "ossification of office" (1999, 77). When a teacher has too little authority in their role as a professional, they are likely to suffer this end. The converse, the insolence of office, which is observable within other, less regulated, professions, like the finance industry, is the result of a professional being granted too much autonomy within their role.

It seems that with no authority other than that of the teachers and the children of Summerhill, there is a distinct risk of the development of the insolence of office which develops as a result of their isolation. Further, without any recognition of a civic culture at all and through a lack of interaction and accountability, there is a risk of young people maintaining this insolence or alienating and isolating themselves once they leave Summerhill and enter the real world. Finally, and intimately connected to this, to have any lasting effect, the model of education that Neill promotes must be universalisable. Otherwise, the tiny minority of self-governing people who develop in a Summerhill-style education system will disappear amongst the masses. This risk is brought to bear by Judith Suissa who writes of Summerhill,

> ... there is little attempt to engage with broader social issues or to confront present socio-political reality. Indeed, there is very much a sense ... of the school having created a little island, in which Summerhill, and the superior kind of education which it represents, is regarded as being against the rest of the world, with its misguided ideas.
>
> (2011, 96)

John Darling raises three further objections. These are specifically objections with Neill's Summerhill, but they are important considerations when exploring the value of internally democratic schooling. Darling's first objection raises the concern that there are employees of Summerhill outside of the teachers and pupils, people who do not live on the grounds but, nevertheless, are affected by the decisions made, most notably the chambermaids. Neill laments over how difficult their job is at Summerhill but is comforted by what he sees as a superior work ethic as a result of the absence of authority over them. Neill writes,

> In Summerhill, we have chambermaids from the town who work for us all day but who sleep in their own homes. They are young girls who work hard and well. In a free atmosphere where they are not bossed, they work harder and better than maids do who are under authority.
>
> (1968, 31)

Darling believes that the exclusion of these members of Summerhill shows that a universal suffrage is not practised and exercises, whether wilfully or not, a class-based system. It is hard to see how he is wrong. It is clear that these people are affected by the decisions and actions of the other members of Summerhill, and yet they do not have a voice, they do not have a democratic presence, and they do not have their interests represented in the model of self-governance so integral to the democratic model of Summerhill.

Second, he considers the undue influence exerted by the adult population of Summerhill. Darling argues that there is a natural authority of learned experience and knowledge that will have an important influence on the outcome of any decision. Therefore, the teachers, and in particular the school head, will exert an influence greater than their equalised voting power. This is because these people will almost always be the most learned and experienced in a dynamic such as the one at Summerhill. Darling argues that some children, the younger especially, will defer to the judgement of their teachers or the older children. If this is the case, then one can extend the argument to suggest that the democracy is only seeming, that a well-skilled headteacher in sophistry and rhetoric will be able to rule the school quite effectively even within the democratic model.

This follows directly into Darling's third objection that a level of centralised and autocratic power exists at Summerhill in spite of the professed freedom and equality. Neill forbade strong drink in the school and writes of how anxious he was whenever a craze for wooden swords began, insisting, "that the points be covered with rubber or cloth" (1968, 34). Further to this, Darling notes that there are certain things that Neill always kept out of the democratic process. His wife planned the bedroom arrangements, and Neill himself appointed and dismissed teachers without assistance or consultation. The question becomes, is it reasonable to have these issues decided democratically with the students, and if not, where should the line be drawn? Additionally, if a line is to be drawn, can it be done so without arbitrariness? This is certainly not clear, but the examples given clearly do affect the members of the Summerhill community, and so by excluding them from these decisions, they represent concrete examples of a clear limitation on the democratic governance of its members.

Responding on behalf of the internally democratic school

I think that it is important to answer Darling's objections first, not because they are more challenging, quite the opposite. Darling's objections highlight inconsistencies in Summerhill but do not refute broadly internally democratic schooling. Arguably, Darling is providing guidance on how to strengthen the principles of the internally democratic school. They are also quite obvious objections, so obvious that Neill anticipated them and addresses them in his work, but he does so primarily through reassurance or empirical observation. However, Darling's concerns warrant a more thorough response.

With regard to the non-residential staff at Summerhill, it is clear that their interests cannot be effectively represented or their voice justifiably silenced in light of the principles of the school. Summerhill operates by direct democracy, and to be effective, it is clear that the ideal number of participants must remain small, but the non-residential staff, both administrative and maintenance, cannot remain voiceless. The obvious answer is to include them in the democratic process, and they will not be a voting block so large as to cause any power imbalance, and correspondingly, the group of eligible voters remains reasonably small. An alternative to this solution is to grant them status more similar to that of a union. Allow them the space to voice their interests through regularly scheduled meetings with the democratic body and work together to ensure a healthy balance. Regardless of the solution offered, it must be one that is coherent with the larger principles of democratic education. For the sake of coherence and accountability, it must be granted that all participants in the school community be included in some meaningful way, thereby ensuring that each school remains both consistent with its principles and autonomous in itself.

Undue influence, on the other hand, needs no modification – although it will always remain an open concern, as it does in local and national democratic politics. It is true that we should always be on the lookout for some "Moses" that wishes to lead us to salvation and can make great impact in virtue of their charisma and sweetened words. But this possibility is exactly the type of circumstance that the internally democratic school aims to prevent through its teaching, and a significant part of this teaching is through the example set by the adults and older students within the community of the school. Therefore, in response to the question of the undue influence of teachers due to their learned position, their eloquence of expression, and their inherent authority, I simply respond: I hope so.

Children are, or at least should be, learning democracy by taking part in democracy; they are learning to rule by ruling. They are self-governing and free from the earliest age, but their competence, influence, and democratic virtues are not borne fully formed. Neill himself recognises that the younger children need the older children present in order to have a well-functioning democracy. Without the guiding influence of the older children, the younger do not take much interest in democracy, but this is not a bad thing; it is a stage of the development of democratic virtues. When those children grow up, they will become the leaders of democracy and have a positive influence on the new generation of younger children. Neill writes, "Free children are not easily influenced; the absence of fear accounts for this phenomenon. Indeed, the absence of fear is the finest thing that can happen to a child" (1968, 24). With this in mind, maybe it is fairer to say that any influence that a teacher or an older child has over another is not the negative influence that we assume it to be but an influence of mutual respect for another free self-governing person.

I aim to resolve the problem of Neill's occasional autocracy through the federalist disestablishment of education and state, which is set out in Chapter 6. This is because in a federalist system, everything is challengeable at some level. The more central a value to the heart of the model of education, the higher the level of appeal in order to have it changed. Therefore, everything that does not undermine the principles protected at the more centralised spheres of governance should be a part of the democratic discussion and protected by the principles of self-governance. This includes timetabling, prohibitions, and the hiring and firing of staff. I do not see this as problematic, and I believe that it effectively dispels any complaint of autocracy because each power is held in check by other powers, and every decision outside of that can be challenged by anyone within the system.

In contrast to Darling, Amy Gutmann does intend to refute the practice of internally democratic schooling, and her objections are designed to achieve this end. However, I do not believe that her objections are successful in this aim. While it is true that by not being funded by the state, the children that frequent schools like Summerhill are much more likely to come from conducive family backgrounds for the successful application of democratic schooling; it is a convenient and ultimately ill-informed dismissal of the theory. It must be remembered that the theory of Summerhill was borne in very different circumstances. Neill was a disciple of Homer Lane whose reformatory, The Little Commonwealth, was designed to cure troubled youths through unconditional love. Summerhill was created in its image after the Little Commonwealth closed down, and Neill did not get the opportunity to teach there as he had hoped. The Little Commonwealth received youth offenders, sentenced in the courts, and was supported by the Home Office. In Summerhill's early years, it gave a home to many young people excluded from conventional education institutions. In many cases, it was their parents' last resort and was not an ideological destination. Neill designed Summerhill on the grounds of a psychological theory for problem children and applied it generally to all children. It is only after establishing itself as a successful school for those young people that parents who shared the philosophy of Summerhill began to send their children there also.

In her second objection, Gutmann leans heavily on our prejudiced view of young people, asserting that they are not capable, that they are not responsible, and that they cannot be trusted. It represents a hasty dismissal of their abilities and one that should give us pause due to its reminiscence to the arguments employed against the unpropertied, women and non-whites. Intuitively one may find themselves agreeing with Gutmann's assessment despite Neill providing numerous empirical observations to the contrary. However, there is a better response than falling into the trap of competing individual examples in an effort to prove a general rule.

We should reconsider Gutmann's assumption because it is self-fulfilling. It is self-fulfilling because it treats people as if they lack certain qualities and then removes from them their powers of self-governance on the basis of that very assumption. In consequence, it takes away the opportunity for people to prove the case to be otherwise and promotes the conclusion it professes by its very practice. We have seen this as an illogical and harmful argument in relation to exclusion of women from education, politics, and the wider public sphere because they lack reason. We have seen this as an illogical and harmful argument in relation to the exclusion of non-whites from education, politics, and the wider public sphere because they are less intelligent. Therefore, we must treat an argument such as this with great suspicion. That young people often fulfil this negative conception of the child is a psychological factor that helps to explain the difference between free and unfree children, in a Neillian sense. However, it is important to note that Neill does temper his account to recognise that children under a certain age show less democratic strength, despite their willing participation. Neill writes, "Children up to, say, twelve, ... will not run good self-government on their own, because they have not reached the social age" (1968, 59–60).

The answer to the inability and shortcomings of young people draws us back to our response to Darling. The influence of the older children in the school maintains the smooth running of the Summerhill GSM, but the younger children through their participation and through their equal status learn the character of those senior students. Senior students were not borne fully formed as democratic leaders but developed through the process of participation. If we choose to exclude some people from participation, we are drawing an arbitrary line, and in doing so, we will not protect democracy but simply delay the development of the skills needed in order to participate effectively and well. In short order, we would find ourselves needing to delay democratic participation still further. Let us not forget that it is not on the grounds of participation and skill that adults are permitted to participate in the democratic process. It is by right and responsibility. It is because they are both subject and citizen. It is because they are a necessary check to governance and because they feel the consequences of decisions made in their daily lives. What here is different for the young person in a school? And what right do we have in changing the goalposts of participation and democratic voice?

The response to Gutmann's third objection is found in combination with the federated disestablishment of education and state of Chapter 6. There is no risk of the insolence of office when internally democratic schooling is instigated across the state school system because the federated model provides a space for the active voice of all interested parties in the education of young people. And the risk is somewhat mitigated by the young people themselves through their own active voice – the professional voice of the teacher is integral, but it is not alone and not held to account through dialogue. Similarly, the young people who graduate from these schools will no longer disappear like Nozick's tomato soup into the ocean for two reasons. It is not just their number that resists this consequence, but it is also their character.

In developing the values that they wish to live by in communion with others and learning how to embody those values, there is little risk of dissipation regardless of number because they will each become leaders – leaders by example.

The reasons that Gutmann rejects models of internally democratic schools are illustrative of an educator's fear of ceding their authority, and parallel arguments are used by defenders of a strong centralised government; defenders of the status quo; and defenders of existing power relations regardless of the disparities between the oppressed and oppressor classes. However, most people will remain disenfranchised for as long as they are treated as such and their powers of self-governance will not develop in an environment where they are simply ruled over, rather than participating in the process of ruling.

Arguments such as those employed by Gutmann have been used by established authority since time immemorial against the suffrage of each successive group fighting for a voice. This alone should make us suspicious of the objection as it has already proven fallacious countless times as suffrage has been extended outside of the nobility, to unpropertied males, to the uneducated, to women, and to minority ethnic populations. Furthermore, Gutmann undermines her own rejection of internally democratic schooling in her discussion of democratic virtue. Gutmann argues that by educating all creeds and classes in the same classroom, "by respecting religious and ethnic differences", through participation and involvement, the students are able to develop and exercise reason and judgement. If, as Gutmann claims, democratic virtues, like the principles of nondiscrimination and nonrepression, can be taught by practising them in the classroom – by teaching black and white children, by teaching Christian and Muslim children, by teaching girls and boys side by side, we can teach the values: "respect among races, religious toleration, patriotism, and political judgment" – then it must be explained why we cannot teach a child how to rule through that child ruling (Gutmann 1999, 63). I believe that if Gutmann's argument is to be consistent, then it must commit to the view that a justifiable way to learn the value of democracy and one's place within a democratic society is by partaking in that democracy directly.

The problem that remains

I believe that these objections to internally democratic schools have been satisfactorily answered and the problem of authority resolved in the response to them. Furthermore, I believe that internally democratic schools provide an effective response to the competing claims on what form the citizen should take. It is through internally democratic schools, through children becoming the authors of their own lives, or through the practice of democracy that they will discover the form of the citizen that they wish to embody. The democracy that is spoken of is not the mere act of voting; it is a Deweyan democracy, a democracy that forms an embryonic community, and a democracy which breaks down the boundaries between school and society. Therefore, the children in their learning are not left without foundations on which to build; they are not left untethered and lost but active and engaged within a local community that will inform their development through existing practice. Yet, through Freirean problem-posing education, these practices will not avoid critique. Conversely, they will provide both the foundations upon which practice and morality is built but also by which it is developed through the continual re-problematisation of the existing state of affairs and dialogue of the community.

However, there is a problem that remains in internally democratic schooling, one that takes us back to the concept of authority. It is seen in the nagging of the adult workers in White Lion Street School. It is seen in the risk of the insolence of office. It is seen lurking underneath the veneer of legitimacy in each model of authority that has been considered. It is the ontological assumption, an assumption which underpins each conception of authority and is rarely discussed.

By the ontological assumption I mean, it is assumed that there is a property of an individual or group which is expressed by that authority over those subject to it. Arendt's conceptualisation of authority incorporates the ontological assumption within her account. This is evidenced by a comparison of the key terms that she offers in *On Violence*. Arendt writes,

> It is, I think, a rather sad reflection on the present state of political science that our terminology does not distinguish among such key words as 'power,' 'strength,' 'force,' 'authority,' and, finally, 'violence' – all of which refer to distinct, different phenomena and would hardly exist if they did.
>
> (1970, 43)

Arendt defines power as the capacity for agents to act in concert for a public–political purpose. Power is legitimated through the medium of speech and persuasion by individuals acting in concert. It is direct and interactive. In virtue of this, it is never the property of an individual, instead, "it belongs to a group and remains in existence only so long as the group keeps together" (Arendt 1970, 44). Therefore, when a person is spoken of as, "being in power", Arendt argues that what is being referred to is the power given to that person by others. They are, "empowered by a certain number of people to act in their name" (Arendt 1970, 44). In contrast to this,

> Strength unequivocally designates something in the singular, an individual entity; it is the property inherent in an object or person and belongs to its character, which may prove itself in relation to other things or persons, but is essentially independent of them.
>
> (Arendt 1970, 44)

Arendt's conceptualisation of authority turns on the idea that authority is expressed when an issued command is followed because that command has been issued by a recognised authority. Therefore, the practice of authority is dependent upon the belief by both the superordinate and the subordinate that the person or institution possesses the authority to make the demands. As such, ontologically, authority sits closer to strength than to power. As stated in Chapter 4, authority is vested in persons or offices. In being "vested" authority is settled or fixed within the person or office to the point that "a priest can grant valid absolution even though he is drunk" (Arendt 1970, 45). Therefore, authority is a property of a person or office that persists in that thing independently of other objects in the same way that an apple may possess the property of "redness" or hydrogen possesses the property of being flammable. In an account of authority such as Arendt's, authority is a property of a person held over others and expressed unilaterally.

Wolff in his conception of authority assumes the same ontological foundation of authority. He remarks,

> ... authority resides in persons; they possess it – if indeed they do at all – by virtue of who they are and not by virtue of what they command. My duty to obey is a duty owed to them, not to the moral law or to the beneficiaries of the actions I may be commanded to perform.
>
> (1998, 6)

In identifying this aspect of authority, Wolff draws out a central tension between authority and freedom from the ontological perspective. He argues that when one acts autonomously, they are not subject to any person's will besides their own, and they remain autonomous even if their action coincides with the command of authority. This was made clear in Chapter 4 in the difference in perspective on authority offered by Raz and Wolff, where the former felt that the thoughts of the subject of authority did not matter, and the latter argued that coinciding reasons meant that one's autonomy was retained. In this way, a person can satisfy the conditions of being politically free even when their actions match the actions of one responding directly to the issued command of authority. In effect, Wolff is arguing that an expression of authority is successful only if the intended subjects of that expression follow it and did so because that individual or group commanded them to do so. Wolff expresses this insight when he writes, "my complying with his command does not constitute an acknowledgment on my part of any such authority" (1998, 6).

In contrast, according to Raz, it simply does not matter whether a person accepts the commands of authority or not. As noted in Chapter 4, he writes, "from the point of view of the person in authority, it is not what the subject thinks but how he acts" (1990, 119). Despite their difference in this matter, both of these views hold fast to the ontological assumption. This is obvious in the case of Raz who cares little for the state of mind of those subject to commands from authority, but it is also true of Wolff.

It may seem to be the case that the state of mind of those subject to authority is integral in an expression of legitimate authority, but it is because of Wolff's acceptance of the ontological assumption that he concludes that autonomy and authority are incompatible. If I were going to act in accordance with a command, I will do so either because I have been commanded and am therefore unfree or because of coinciding reasons and therefore not subject to authority. In Wolff's formulation, even in instances of mindful acquiescence, there has been no legitimate authority because authority is a unilateral expression over others.

Friedrich offers a slight shift in this perspective because the ontology of authority moves from the object of authority to the communication by that object. It is in the communication that authority is found, but that communication is rooted in the potentiality of reasoned deliberation. This is an unquestioned and assumed quality of a person or office to issue authoritative commands. It is for this reason that Friedrich perceives authority as a property of a person's communication and not of the person themselves. Therefore, Friedrich is also guilty of the ontological assumption.

This is the case for Weber as well, according to whom, authority is a type of power distinct from coercive power. Yet in both cases, power is understood as an imposition of will over others. Weber notes that, "a certain minimum of voluntary submission" is a condition of authority (1978, 324). Weber argues that if incentives of threats are employed to illicit compliance, then authority has not been exercised. Blau writes that Weber's conceptualisation of authority, "is distinguished from persuasion by the fact that people *a priori* suspend their own judgment and accept that of an acknowledged superior without having to be convinced that this is correct" (1963, 307). Therefore, while authority is the result of the beliefs of those subject to authority, it is clear that for Weber, authority is a property of a person or office which, in virtue of those beliefs, is expressed unilaterally over a subordinate group.

The ontological assumption also appears clearly in educational theory. It is clear in the Weberian conception of authority offered by Metz as well as by Peters. Additionally, Nyberg and Farber incorporate Friedrich's conception of authority into their educational theory. They write,

> Authority is a term of internal relation; it is a matter of getting other people interested in doing or believing what you want without using force or rational argument. However, to say this is not to say that authority is unrelated to reason and rational argument. It helps to understand this point if we think of authority as "a quality of communication, rather than of persons," and think of authoritative persons as those who possess "the capacity to issue authoritative communication."
>
> (1986, 7)

What this means is that unilateral conceptions of authority either impose their will on those subject to that authority without consideration of any private judgement or independent action, thereby denying an individual the freedom to choose otherwise or to rely upon their own judgement: or, they simply miss their intended targets, and while those subjects may have acted according to their own reason or autonomously, they have acted contrary to authority. Therefore, unilateral conceptions of authority are seemingly in irresolvable conflict with reason and freedom, and defenders of such conceptions must either accept this incompatibility or offer an explanation which shows otherwise. This is the mistake that models of democratic education make by not adequately considering the voice of the young people themselves.

Relational authority

In educational theory, a radical re-evaluation of the ontology of authority is taking place. Authors such as Charles Bingham (2008), Nicolas C. Burbules (1995, 2004), and Barbara Applebaum (1999) offer examples of this approach to authority. The conceptual idea that authority is a property of a person, institution, or role is being challenged by the idea that authority is instead a relation. The difference is that a property of a thing persists in that thing independently of other objects. Whereas a relation of a thing persists only in relation to other things. For example, a red apple possesses the property of "redness" but possesses the relation of "larger than" only in relation to a smaller thing. Freire's conception of authority in *Pedagogy of the Oppressed* challenges the idea that authority is a property of a person or institution in this sense and that legitimate authority must be understood dialogically and in relation with freedom.

Bingham argues in favour of understanding authority relationally, rather than possessively. Bingham develops his understanding of the ontology of authority from the politico-educational project of Paulo Freire. Freire argues that the role of the teacher must be recast and understood anew. According to Freire's pedagogical method, problem-posing education, no longer is the teacher the possessor of knowledge and the students empty vessels to be filled. Instead, the teacher is a teacher-student, and the students are students-teachers. Together through dialogical exchange, they learn and teach together in reciprocation. Freire writes,

> The teacher is no longer merely the one-who-teaches, but one who is himself taught in dialogue with the students, who in turn while being taught also teach. They become jointly responsible for a process in which all grow. In this process, arguments based on "authority" are no longer valid; in order to function, authority must be *on the side of* freedom, not *against* it.
>
> (2017, 53)

However, Bingham raises two concerns with respect to the coherence of the conception of authority employed by Freire within his politico-educational project. Bingham argues that the conception of authority presented in Freire's philosophy is confused. According to Bingham, Freire presents a monological account of authority because he fails to escape the perceived dichotomy between authority and freedom within the dominant philosophical tradition. This happens in two ways. First, he retains the use of the terms that are at stake. While Freire offers a response to the problem of authority, Bingham argues that Freire continues to use the terms with the same definition as the dominant tradition to which his theory objects. Bingham writes, "He refutes the mutually exclusive nature of authority and freedom, but does not provide any nuance for understanding the difference between the two" (2008, 135). Freire perceives a false dichotomy in authority and freedom yet assumes the definition of authority as a property possessed by an individual or group over another individual or group.

The second problem that Bingham identifies with Freire's conception of authority is that his solution of the dichotomy is reconciliation by fiat (Bingham 2008, 134–135). Bingham refers to Freire's claim in *Pedagogy of the Oppressed* that authority will be on the side of freedom. Bingham claims that there is no substantive difference between authority on the side of freedom and banking education being used as an interim measure in the revolution, something Freire expressly denies the possibility of. Therefore, there is no account of, "what authority actually does once it is on the side of freedom" (Bingham 2008, 135).

Bingham is one example of a group of education theorists who have recently attempted to redefine authority and break with a tradition which has persistently perceived authority as a quality possessed by a person or group which is expressed over another person or group. Instead of authority existing as a property of an individual that is unilaterally expressed, they argue that one ought to understand authority as relational. Bingham describes authority as,

> ... enacted in circuits where each participant has a role to play, where authority is not simply a monological enactment, where it takes the participation of at least two people for authority to gain purchase. It works as a circuit instead of working unidirectionally or monologically.
>
> (2008, 6–7)

Echoing these words, Burbules writes that authority is,

> ... a *relational* concept, arising from the particular bonds or respect, concern, and trust that particular teachers and students establish among themselves. Authority in this sense exists neither before nor beyond the interactions, communicative and otherwise, that join two or more parties in a relation of mutuality and shared interest.
>
> (1995, 36)

Lastly, Applebaum addresses relational authority motivated by the project of discovering the model of authority consonant with her role as feminist educator. Applebaum writes, "My primary purpose is to recommend a reconceptualization of authority, which I refer to as 'relational authority,' that can, I maintain, dissolve the sharp dichotomy between nurturance and authority that [Carmen] Luke and other feminists embrace" (1999, 307). Applebaum challenges the patriarchal dichotomisation in educational practice between "authority" and "nurturance". She argues that maternal nurturance is perceived in opposition to masculine power and authority, "the masculinist tradition of education has similarities to what Neiman, following Peters, describes as a necessary feature of education, namely, the socio-political authority of the teacher" (1999, 309). In her analysis, Applebaum identifies two types of authority: the control and command model of authority, and the influence and inspire model of authority. The difference between the two, according to Applebaum, is that the former, "implies unidirectional encounters while the latter intimates reciprocal experiences and relationships" (Applebaum 1999, 314).

In redefining authority, Burbules, Bingham, and Applebaum have provided a platform to escape the dichotomy between authority and freedom which is inherent within the dominant conception of authority. In understanding authority as relational, it is no longer a property possessed by the teacher which is then expressed through their presence and their commands. This is because relational authority does not issue from one person or group but is instead offered and accepted by object and subject alike. It is earned through interaction. A teacher gains authority, according to Burbules, in two ways. First, it is essential to recognise the impact of their role upon their students and respond to it and, "encourage students to question it" (Burbules 1995, 34). Second, it is in, "acknowledging differences in knowledge, experience, or ability without reifying them" (Burbules 1995, 38). This allows for relational authority to remain fluid rather than fixed over time because in the honest and dialogical environment being encouraged through this model of authority, there, "manifests reciprocity and respect by who listens as well as by who speaks" (Burbules 1995, 38). Over time, Burbules argues that a relationship built on these foundations may lead to the dissolution of authority between the participants of that relationship.

Conclusion

In this chapter, I have provided a defence of internally democratic schooling in the face of objections by Amy Gutmann and John Darling. I was then able to show that even after each of these objections had been responded to, a significant problem remained, one that was related to the persistent problem of authority.

It is ultimately a mistake to try and dissolve authority, but it is also a mistake to attempt to square authority with freedom. The reason for this seemingly irresolvable conflict is found at the heart of all major conceptualisations of authority, an ontological assumption that has remained largely unquestioned and unchallenged. This assumption is that authority is the property of a person or group of people which is then expressed over another person or group of people; it is a unilateral and monological property, and in its expression, it commands those who do not possess that property to obey.

A relational conception of authority is the alternative and the key that can open the door to a functioning and dynamic model of democratic education with internally democratic schools at its core. It can do this because it achieves something that Rousseau's tutor and Lawgiver were transgressors of, that Dewey's epistemically authoritative teachers were transgressors of, and that Freire's revolutionary leaders were transgressors of. It offers a realisation of a freedom that works in concert with authority because authority is no longer a property of a person or group that is imposed on others but is instead a shared relation between persons. It is a thing that is granted within a certain context and limited to a certain scope that is understood by the requisite parties in virtue of the relationship that they have with one another.

There is, of course, room for error and the existence of disjunctive relations, but this does not negate them entirely – its legitimacy is found in the shared consent and ends where disagreement begins. I may think that I have been granted authority by a student of mine in virtue of our relationship to comment and offer advice or guidance on their private life. If I am mistaken and that student grants authority to me only in a much more limited manner, only as far as my teaching responsibilities permit for example, then any discussion of their personal affairs is an expression of illegitimate authority. This may seem obvious, but it is contrary to our common understanding of authority as a value held unilaterally. In such understandings, my comments may be considered inappropriate but not necessarily illegitimate.

Authority as a property that is earned through reciprocal relationships is fertile ground for an active and true democracy of individuals who wish to express their freedom by participating in a world with other people. In the conclusion of this book, I shall humour my fantasies and indulge in a picture of what this might look like.

Note

1 Not to be confused or conflated with free schools in the contemporary sense which are schools funded by the government but not run by the local authority. These schools are not run according to the principles of the free school movement, although hypothetically at least a free school could be a free school. They are run by any set of principles that the Department of Education approves.

References

Applebaum, Barbara. 1999. 'On Good Authority or Is Feminist Authority an Oxymoron?' *Philosophy of Education Archive*, 307–17.
Arendt, Hannah. 1970. *On Violence*. New York: Harcourt, Brace & World.

Bingham, Charles W. 2008. *Authority Is Relational: Rethinking Educational Empowerment*. Albany: State University of New York Press.

Blau, Peter M. 1963. 'Critical Remarks on Weber's Theory of Authority'. *American Political Science Review* 57 (02): 305–16.

Burbules, Nicholas C. 1995. 'Authority and the Tragic Dimension of Teaching'. In *The Educational Conversation: Closing the Gap*, edited by James W. Garrison and Anthony G. Rud, 29–40. SUNY Series, the Philosophy of Education. Albany: State University of New York Press.

Burbules, Nicholas C. 2004. 'Response: Some Dilemmas of Teacher Authority'. *Philosophy of Education Archive*, 205–8.

Freire, Paulo. 2017. *Pedagogy of the Oppressed*. Translated by Myra Bergman Ramos. London: Penguin Books.

Gutmann, Amy. 1999. *Democratic Education*. Princeton, NJ; Chichester: Princeton University Press.

Neill, Alexander Sutherland. 1968. *Summerhill*. Pelican Books. Harmondsworth; Middlesex: Penguin Books.

Nyberg, David, and Paul Farber. 1986. 'Authority in Education'. *Teachers College Record* 88 (1): 4–14.

Raz, Joseph. 1990. 'Authority and Justification'. In *Authority*, edited by Joseph Raz, 115–41. Readings in Social and Political Theory. Oxford: Basil Blackwell.

Suissa, Judith. 2011. *Anarchism and Education: A Philosophical Perspective*. Oakland: PM Press.

Weber, Max. 1978. *Economy and Society: An Outline of Interpretive Sociology*. Edited by Guenther Roth and Claus Wittich. Berkeley: University of California Press.

Wolff, Robert Paul. 1998. *In Defense of Anarchism*. Berkeley: University of California Press.

Wright, Nigel. 1989a. *Assessing Radical Education: A Critical Review of the Radical Movement in English Schooling, 1960–1980*. Innovations in Education. Milton Keynes; Philadelphia, PA: Open University Press.

Wright, Nigel.1989b. *Free School: The White Lion Experience*. Leicestershire, England: Libertarian Education.

Conclusion

Concluding remarks

In this book, I have attempted to bring education into the centre of political discourse. Instead of engaging in ideal theory where I can construct the present-day utopia, or of engaging in non-ideal theory where I take the imperfect political world and modify it for an imperfect political individual, I have attempted to offer a methodology that is capable of moving us from our flawed and corrupted starting place and moving us towards a utopia without force or coercion. It is surely naïve but a naïveté that I embrace.

In this conclusion, I shall in the first instance review the argument that I have made to this point. Then, I shall attempt to temper expectations by reiterating the intentionally vague conclusions drawn. Finally, I shall bite the bullet and express my imaginings of the federated disestablishment of education and state and of internally democratic schooling. This can be treated as the opening stimulus for what I hope will lead to a rigorous critical reconstruction.

The argument so far

In Chapter 1, I established the methodology that underpins the political and educational approach of this book. It is through the legacy and example set by Jean-Jacques Rousseau, John Dewey, and Paulo Freire that the arguments contained throughout this book are motivated. What we learn from them is that the political question is an educational one, that it is through education that we can develop the tools, skills, and strength necessary for cooperative association, and it is through education that our cooperative association can grow and begin to make decisions for the well-being of the people under its dominion and not for its own self-preservation. However, in addition to this, we learnt from Rousseau the importance of addressing the tension between the individual and society from both the institutional and interactional perspective and that it is only when these two prongs are pursued in concert that an answer can be given; we learnt from Dewey the importance of the relationship between means and ends in the realisation of the aims that we identify;

DOI: 10.4324/9781003271871-9

and we learnt from Freire the dialogical framework upon which together we will be able to challenge and re-interpret the world in which we live.

In Chapter 2, through an analysis of the citizen, I identified the model of the citizen that represents the end-in-view of this political and educational endeavour. I promoted a citizen which is descriptively communitarian, normatively cosmopolitan, an active participant in one's society, and a possessor of both rights and responsibilities. This person I call the Critical Citizen. In Chapter 3, I then establish the problem that I aim to address with the method of Chapter 1 in order to create the citizen of Chapter 2. It is here that I introduce the problem of authority as the key issue in the tension between the individual and society.

In Chapters 4 and 5, I offer a two-part analysis of the problem of authority: first, within the context of the institutional structure of education and, second, from within the context of the interactional structure of education. Then, in the final two chapters of this book, I respond to the most important objections to democratic education and its ability in offering an answer to the problem of authority both at the institutional and interactional levels. I then posit the federated disestablishment of education and state and internally democratic schooling as the two key solutions to the problem of authority and the tension between the individual and society.

Radicalism and moderation

The conclusions that I have drawn are both radical and yet moderate. They are moderate because they are by all accounts reasonable conclusions reached from an analysis of political and educational theories of authority. They do not demand the destruction of the world, and they do not justify the continued oppression of people in a state like this. They acknowledge a certain intractability of freedom and authority but do not prioritise one over the other. Instead, they embrace the tension and see it as the key motivating force for change. It is in the interplay between freedom and authority, as people struggle for their voice and their stability, that we are to find the resolution of the tension between the individual and society, and in turn the problem of authority. This is therefore a moderate conclusion that I draw because I seek not to reject authority in the name of freedom or to constrain freedom in the name of order and responsibility. I wish to keep them both in competition with each other so that we continue to fight for better.

However, the conclusion that I draw is also radical and represents a difficult position for some to entertain. This is because my proposal would require the large-scale reorganisation of society, both in relationships with each other and how we choose to engage with the society of which we are a part, as well as in the institutional framework of that society. It is radical because it demands a complete reversal of how we normally construe our role as adults in society. No longer should we be the elders who know better, ready to guide and instruct the next generation in the moral, social, and political success that we are responsible for. No longer are we to elevate a world such as this as a representation of the inexorable progress of the human animal. No longer are we to fight to maintain the existing values and understandings, trapped in the betrayal of the principle of self-preservation. Instead, we are to cede some of our authority and share it with those people we are wont to control, those people who are still in the process of being formed, those people whose corrupted form has not yet taken hold. It is the emancipation of the young and giving them the space, the tools, and the social environment necessary to discover both the person whom they want to be and the society that they wish to live in, that is radical in my conclusion.

What I offer is not intended as the answer to the tension between the individual and society but an expression of the conditions that would allow for a continued exploration by all of the people subject to the tension, subject to authority, and subject to the constraints on their freedom. In the remainder of this conclusion, I shall attempt to visualise in more detail what this environment could look like. Although it must be noted that this in itself must be subject to change as well and cannot be treated as outside of the methodological process that is designed to provide the space for people to realise their individual and societal freedom.

Federated disestablishment of education and state

The form of disestablishment that should be sort is not obvious because there are two competing risks; its construct must protect the independence of the body from undue influence, and it must also be subject to checks and measures on its authority.

There are institutions already in the United Kingdom that are funded by the government but operate independently of them. Good examples of these are the British Broadcasting Corporation, the Bank of England, some museums and galleries such as the V&A and the Tate galleries, and most recently Oak National Academy. In each of these instances, the institutions are accountable to the public via parliament, and each of them is governed by people who are, at least in part, appointed by the government. However, these institutions are not democratic in structure (Durose et al. 2015). Their independence is questioned on account of the fact that their funding is dependent upon governmental support, and the head of the institution is often appointed directly by them. Furthermore, government officials can and do exert threatening influence over the arm's-length organisations to suit their political ends (Dan Hicks 2020). Ultimately, there is little in the way of checks and measures outside of the pressure exerted by members of the legislative and executive bodies.

The disestablishment that I imagine is not too dissimilar to these models, but it does differ in that it is placed within a federal structure that stretches from the classroom all the way through to the boardroom. At the top level, the governing body of education is a national body and will be constructed with members of each interested party. Therefore, there will be members appointed by the government who are elected into their position by the citizenry, and these people will represent the interests of the state and the citizenry; there will be members who are elected by school governors who represent the interests of parents; there will be members elected by the education institutions, who will represent the interest of those schools, colleges, and universities; there will be members of the teacher unions who will be elected by the teachers and represent the interests of professional standards. Finally, there will be members elected by the young people themselves and represent the interests of the student body.

In order to avoid the dominance of one voice, these disparate groups should be weighted according to the degree of interest that they have in the means and ends of education. It seems clear that the young people themselves have the greatest interest and therefore should have the greatest representation in the national body. Similarly, the professional educators, the schools themselves, and the parents of the young people in education have a much greater interest in education than the citizenry and the state. But that does not mean that the general citizenry and the state do not have an interest at all, and they should have the space to participate in this political body.

With this in mind, I imagine a political body at the national level of 60, or multiples thereof, with the following proportional representation: one-third of the members are representatives of the student body; one-quarter of the members are representatives of the professional educators; one-sixth of the members are representatives of headteachers of the schools, colleges, and universities across the country; a further sixth of the members are parent governors and representatives of the interests of parents; lastly, one-twelfth of the body are members of parliament and appointed by the government. This would translate as twenty student representatives, fifteen professional educators, ten headteachers, ten parent governors, and five members of parliament for every sixty members of the federal body.

This is a relatively small body, and I have selected the number 60 due more to its mathematical properties than for any political or geographical reasons. The advantage that it gives is found in its easy divisibility, thereby providing proportionate representation for each democratic voice and ensuring that the representatives of any group will not be in a position to dominate any other. Each group will be large enough to be able to form alliances and voting blocks. So, decisions should be able to be made in most circumstances. Yet the scope of this body is limited by the federal structure. So, even if, for a short time, a group do dominate, their authority is checked at the other levels of that federated structure. As Gutmann (1999) suggests, the scope of the national level should be limited to ensuring the levels of governance below them adhere to the principles of nondiscrimination and nonrepression, and assessing the democratic competence of those levels. To avoid an undermining of democracy, I would suggest a two-third rule for matters of override, which requires at least forty members for every sixty within the body to vote in favour of the override for it to pass.

The national body feeds into and is fed from the regional level of the educational structure. Similar to the national level, I see five broad groups with varying degrees of direct interest in educational matters and foresee it being constructed in the same way with the same proportional representation. This in turn, depending on the size and complexity of the cooperative association, may lead to a local federal level. This will share a structure similar to those above it. However, in this instance, alongside the one-third student representatives and one-quarter representatives of the teacher unions, one-sixth of this body will be members of the senior leadership teams and headteachers of schools in the local area and a further sixth of parent governors from the local area. Lastly, one-twelfth of the local school body will be made up of local council who will represent the political interest of the broader citizenry and the political body they represent.

Therefore, the only significant difference between these three layers of the federal structure is who will be a representative for each group at each of these levels. For example, at the national level, we will see nationally elected members of parliament as the representatives of the citizenry and the state. Whereas at the regional level, I would expect the representatives of the citizenry and the state to be Regional Assembly members, from the Welsh and Scottish Parliament or the Northern Ireland Assembly, for example, and at the local level, we will see local councillors take on this role.

Internally democratic schooling

I envisage two school levels of federalism below the national, regional, and local levels. These levels concern the particular running of any one school. These two levels of the federal system bridge the gap between the institutional structure and interactional structure of education. At the higher "inter-school" level, I see the need for four interested parties to be represented: the parents, the education institutions, the teachers, and the young people themselves. At this level, the scope of authority is over the whole individual school and will be of slightly different proportions as a result. Working again with base sixty, the inter-school level is made up of four-tenths the young people in the school, three-tenths the teachers of the school, two-tenths the senior leadership team of the school, and one-tenth the parent governors.

The final layer of the federal system is the smallest in scope. Its concerns are the day-to-day rules and relationships of the school class. This is the foundational democratic space and where most people will learn the skills, values, and character that will form the foundation of each subsequent layer. There need to be only three groups that are represented at this "intra-school" level: the young people, the teachers, and the senior leadership team.

It is here, at the intra-school level, where we must be able to make mistakes, experiment with ideas, and learn from the ideas of others more so than at any other democratic sphere. We are the least embedded in our outlook and the most easily led, and as such, this is the place to cultivate new ideas and ways of looking at the world. This is the most fertile ground for democracy, and it must be embraced.

It is in the inter-school and intra-school levels of the federated disestablishment of education and state that the internally democratic school takes shape. Every child from the beginning of their formal education will be involved in decision-making for themselves and their peers, decision-making that will impact directly on their education – this is not to be a hand-waving exercise. This is designed to take Deweyan principles of progressive education seriously and allow schools to be guided by the interests of the young people that make up that community and give it a formal structure, thereby making democracy and participation explicit rather than couching them in the observations and discussions of professionals.

More than this, where it is appropriate, it is an education defined and discovered through dialogue with one's peers in a model of problem-posing education that comes directly from Freire's playbook. The teacher will observe and then present stimuli to children in different learning opportunities. In my own experience, working with children as young as three years old, valuable insight and reflection can take place through discussion, play, and arts and crafts. In response to learning stimuli that is relevant to their lives – concepts such as fairness, private property, and moral goodness are not beyond very many people. Nor are philosophical concepts like sameness, identity, and essential and accidental properties. It is my view that even very young people are capable of producing real insight, but more than that, it is my view that the practice and observation of reflection and analysis are the primary methods for developing the skills of reflection and analysis. An education like this does not discriminate against fact-based subjects, but instead, it cultivates a different and equally valuable model of intelligence that sits alongside them because facts do not have value, and we must be able to interpret and infer knowledge from facts. Otherwise, those facts are at best meaningless and at worst the foundation for dangerous and misguided values like social Darwinism and eugenics.

The democracy I propose is supported by a mentor system that filters through the whole democratic model. At the beginning of our democratic practice in the intra-school level, where the decisions and guidelines of each class are governed, the young people will be supported by their peers from the year above them. Following the example set by Summerhill over the last one hundred years, at each formal meeting where rules are to be voted on and punishments for transgressions to those rules decided, the young people will have not merely adults to act as their guide but other more experienced young people who will lead by example and act as a model of democratic participation

(Brighouse 2006). This will be the case throughout formal education, and as such, schools will need to form relationships with each other so that secondary school students will attend year five and six primary school students' weekly school meetings. Colleges and universities will operate similarly by sending elected advocates to support the democracy of those young people who are learning to find their voice, as we all will continue to do throughout the course of our lives.

In addition to this threaded model of democracy, I envisage training courses will be devised for all interested parties to encourage active participation in the democratic process for education as we learn to take ownership of our lives and let go of our fear of change. It is in short a great revolution of education that will lead to the revolution of the human animal as its malleable psychology bends, not to the will of a denaturing society but to the will of its beneficiaries – each individual will operate as a part of a collective project.

Final words

This sketch, while fantastical, highlights how this model of political philosophy answers the tension between the individual and society, the problem of authority, and the emancipation of the young. It has not dissolved authority, and it has not allowed freedom to disfigure into license. It has instead turned political and educational models on their head and encouraged the development of the person and the institutional support for that aim – and it has done this with a series of checks and measures designed to ensure that change does not occur too fast. Political stability is promoted, and morally objectionable decisions are protected against. There is no call for the immediate abolition of state apparatus, and there is no call for the centralisation of power into the hands of fictions like the Lawgiver or the tutor. There is no need to worry about decisions we cannot be trusted not to make, decisions fuelled by self-interest, prejudice, or self-destruction. We are protected through the federal model and educated so that one day we shall not need it.

References

Brighouse, Harry. 2006. 'Introduction'. In *Summerhill and A. S. Neill*, edited by Mark Vaughan and Tim Brighouse. Maidenhead: Open University Press.

Dan Hicks. 2020. 'The UK Government Is Trying to Draw Museums into a Fake Culture War'. *The Guardian*, 15 October 2020.

Durose, Catherine, Jonathan Justice, and Chris Skelcher. 2015. 'Governing at Arm's Length: Eroding or Enhancing Democracy?' *Policy & Politics* 43 (1): 137–53.

Gutmann, Amy. 1999. *Democratic Education*. Princeton, NJ; Chichester: Princeton University Press.

Index